IMAGES of America
BUFFALO RADIO

In 1996, a group of like-minded broadcasters came together to establish the Buffalo Broadcasting Pioneers, now the Buffalo Broadcasters Association. The mission of the organization was to preserve the rich history of Buffalo's radio and television industry and to promote quality broadcasting into the future. Pictured are the founding board of director members. They are, from left to right, Al Wallack, Jack Sharpe, Al Anscombe, Jim Fagan, Marty Biniasz, John Zach, Don Angelo, Steve Mitchell, Herb Flemming, and Tom Atkins. (Author's collection.)

ON THE COVER: Handsome, youthful, and immensely popular with young female radio listeners, WKBW's Tommy Shannon was a surefire teen heartthrob on Buffalo's "sock hop" circuit in the late 1950s and early 1960s. Shannon's seven-to-midnight show blanketed the entire East Coast of the United States. "KB's" powerful 50,000-watt signal helped to grow his popularity and success outside of the immediate Western New York radio market. In 1964, he would leave his hometown of Buffalo to become a legendary personality in Detroit at Top 40 powerhouse CKLW. Tom Shannon was inducted into the Buffalo Broadcasting Hall of Fame in 2001. He passed away on May 27, 2021. (Author's collection.)

Martin Biniasz

Copyright © 2022 by Martin Biniasz
ISBN 978-1-4671-0636-8

Published by Arcadia Publishing
Charleston, South Carolina

Printed in the United States of America

Library of Congress Control Number: 2022934153

For all general information, please contact Arcadia Publishing:
Telephone 843-853-2070
Fax 843-853-0044
E-mail sales@arcadiapublishing.com
For customer service and orders:
Toll-Free 1-888-313-2665

Visit us on the Internet at www.arcadiapublishing.com

To the pioneers of Buffalo radio, who, for over 100 years, brought our community closer together. By the power of your voice, you made us laugh, brought us the news, became our evening companion, and made our sports heroes come alive.

Contents

Acknowledgments — 6

Introduction — 7

1. WGR — 9
2. WEBR — 31
3. WBEN — 49
4. WKBW — 75
5. Tiny Tots of the Kilowatt — 107

Acknowledgments

Sincere appreciation is given to all the veteran Buffalo broadcasters who spent time sharing their stories and memories. Early in my career, these men were kind, supportive, and nurturing of my efforts in radio and television. Over the years, I was proud to call the likes of Al Wallack, Ed Little, Tom Jolls, Tom Shannon, Jim Fagan, Al Anscombe, Steve Mitchell, Danny Neaverth, Hank Nevins, Tom McCray, Lou Schriver, and Herb Flemming friends. You are my heroes in the industry.

Many individuals have contributed to the preservation and documentation of Buffalo radio history. Among those who laid a strong foundation of information are John Zach, Aaron Heverin, Bob Koshinski, Gary Deeb, Al Anscombe, Danny McBride, and George Thomas Apfel.

A special thank-you goes to Steve Cichon, who, for many years, was my "partner in crime" in saving Buffalo broadcasting history. Together, we learned the art of "dumpster diving" that led to the rescue of key relics and ephemera from the landfill so that future generations would never forget the history of the pioneers who went before us.

I don't want to forget my parents, Patrick and Joann Biniasz, for supporting my love of radio as a child by driving me to countless remote broadcasts, broadcasting internships, and station promotions. Thank you to my wife Kimberly, daughter Katharine, and son Teddy, who tolerate my ever-present piles of ephemera, totes of filled with history, and a storage room dedicated to my "treasures."

All images not specifically credited are from the author's collection.

Introduction

First considered little more than a novelty, radio grew into one of the greatest technological marvels of the 20th century. During the first years of commercial radio broadcasting, it seemed like everyone, including religious leaders, newspapers, schools, manufacturers, and retailers all wanted to get into the business of broadcasting. In 1922, the Department of Commerce and Labor granted the first broadcasting license in Buffalo to prominent electrical equipment dealer McCarthy Bros. & Ford. The firm hoped to use the station as a way to encourage the sale of home radio sets.

On April 16, 1922, WWT went on the air from the McCarthy Bros. Building at 75 West Mohawk Street. With an aerial atop the Niagara Life Building, the first program consisted of an address by Buffalo mayor Francis X. Schwab and an Easter greeting from Rev. George Frederic Williams, rector of St. Mary's-on-the-Hill Episcopal Church. Edward D. O'Dea had the privilege of being Buffalo's first announcer. WWT only broadcast for a few hours at a time and on an irregular basis. After only two months of intermittent broadcasts, WWT's programming became sporadic due to transmitting issues. By October 2, 1922, WWT officially ceased operations permanently.

While WWT struggled to provide a dedicated schedule of broadcasts, experimental station 8XAD, owned by the Federal Telephone & Telegraph Company, began limited broadcasting on a wavelength of 485 meters. The company received its broadcast license on March 14, 1922, and was randomly assigned the call letters WGR. Studios and transmitting equipment were inside the company's sprawling complex in North Buffalo located at 1738 Elmwood Avenue.

On May 22, 1922, 8XAD officially sign-on the air as WGR to become Buffalo's first radio station to offer uninterrupted commercial service to Western New York. WGR's inaugural broadcast included an address and prayer by Rev. Michael Ahern, president of Canisius College, and a concert by the Yankee Six Orchestra. In 1923, WGR would move its operations to the newly constructed Statler Hotel, located on Niagara Square, and then to the Rand Building in 1929.

In Niagara County, I.R. "Ike" Lounsberry of Lockport's Norton Laboratories established WMAK with an experimental signal on September 22, 1922. Although WMAK's broadcasting schedule was limited to a few hours a week, the station's powerful signal could be heard as far as Nevada, according to a story in the October 31, 1922, edition of the *Buffalo Evening News*. Studios were located on Mill Street and then moved to Lockport's Rialto Theater. The station again moved to downtown Buffalo in September 1925 to the Lafayette hotel. WMAK's transmitter and towers were located in Martinsville on Shawnee Road, just north of Niagara Falls Boulevard. WMAK would also call the Liberty Bank Building and the Rand Building home before ending broadcast operations in 1930.

The city of Buffalo's second "licensed" radio station, WEBR, signed on the airwaves October 14, 1924. Owned by Herbert H. Howell's Howell Electric Company, the station was located inside the company's building at the corner of Niagara and Franklin Streets. Given sequentially issued call letters, Howell adopted the slogan "We Extend Buffalo's Regards." The station grew rapidly from the backroom of the Howell Building; it shifted operations to the Gerrans Building at Main and Eagle Streets, the Hotel Worth, 50 West Eagle Street, and 735 Main Street before taking over a formal residential mansion at 23 North Street in 1935. Broadcasting House, as it was known, would be the station's longtime home until 1993.

On December 30, 1925, WPDQ was signed on by Hirman Turner, manager of Norwood Garage, and financed by its president, Nelson P. Baker. Norwood was a pioneer motor livery service specializing in chauffeured luxury automobiles. The station's studios and transmitter were located inside the company's garage, which was located behind a home at 121 Norwood Avenue. On June 10, 1927, WPDQ became WKEN, and a month later, it moved its location from the Varsity Theater on Bailey Avenue to East Hazeltine Avenue in Kenmore. WKEN was owned and operated by the Kenmore Presbyterian Church under the direction of its pastor Rev. John Richelsen.

WGR was indirectly instrumental in bringing about the establishment of one of Buffalo's most storied station, WKBW. A few months after WGR began broadcasting, its station manager invited Dr. Clinton H. Churchill, then pastor of a small congregation on Lafayette Avenue, to bring his church choir to the studio. When bushel baskets full of mail, including envelopes filled with money, came pouring in, the young pastor began to see the potential of radio to grow his congregation. Churchill applied for a noncommercial radio permit with the call letters WAY. In 1926, he was randomly assigned the call letters WKBW, which Churchill quickly translated into "Well Known Bible Witness."

Operating a radio station was not without its financial risks. Quickly changing technology, the energy needed to power transmitting equipment, and programming expenditures were all costly. In less than a year operating under a noncommercial license, Dr. Churchill faced a $90,000 deficit. To solve this financial crisis, Churchill joined forces with a group of local investors and formed the Buffalo Broadcasting Company. The BBC, as it was commonly known, went about consolidating stations in 1928 with the purchase of WGR, WKEN, and WMAK. WKBW was leased from the Churchill Tabernacle for a term of 99-years and received a commercial broadcasting license and a substantial increase in power.

In 1931, the Federal Radio Commission ruled that the BBC's four-station group was not in the best interest of the community and would have to break up its near-monopoly, WKEN was taken off the air, and WMAK was sold to the *Buffalo Evening News*. Further pressure to break up the BBC's two station group resulted in the selling of WGR for $750,000 in 1946 to a group of investors that included Leo Fitzpatrick from Detroit and I.R. Lounsberry. The BBC looked to retain the more powerful WKBW, but Clinton Churchill claimed property rights and began to pursue sole ownership of the station through the establishment of the Broadcasting Foundation, Inc. In 1947, after 16 years under the control of the BBC, WKBW was sold for $375,000, which equaled compensation for capital improvements.

Buffalo newspapers were eager to capitalize on the new medium to promote circulation and civic good will. As early as 1923, both the *Buffalo Evening News* and the *Buffalo Courier-Express* sponsored the broadcasting of concerts, lectures, and news reports. The *Buffalo Courier-Express* strategically aligned itself with WMAK in 1928 before purchasing WEBR in 1942. The *Buffalo Courier-Express*'s primary competitor, *Buffalo Evening News*, would sign-on WBEN in 1930.

WMAK went dark as the result of the Buffalo Broadcasting Corporation breakup but returned to the air on September 8, 1930, under the call letters WBEN (*Buffalo Evening News*). *Buffalo Evening News* wasted no time in capitalizing on the new technology. Modern studios were constructed on the northeastern wing of the Statler Hotel's 18th floor. At 7:00 p.m. on September 8, the strains of "The Star-Spangled Banner" marked the initial presentation of WBEN operating at 900 kilocycles.

On the eve of World War II, nearly 20 years after Buffalo was granted it first radio license, the pioneer era of broadcasting was over. The industry had matured into an important part of the Western New York economy, employing hundreds and generating wealth for its owners. The war years would solidify radio as a vital entertainment and communication link, but VJ Day would signal a decline. Waiting in the wings, ready to be thrust upon postwar consumers, would be television, and Buffalo radio would never be the same. On December 1, 1941, the Buffalo radio dial, excluding Canadian radio stations looked as follows: WGR 550, WBEN 930, WHLD 1260, WEBR 1340, WBNY 1400, and WKBW 1520.

One

WGR

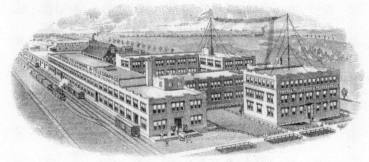

On May 22, 1922, the Federal Telephone and Telegraph Company, located at 1738 Elmwood Avenue in North Buffalo, signed on its radio station WGR. Founded in 1908, Buffalo was the location of Federal's home office and primary factory with support branches in New York City, San Francisco, Chicago, Boston, Philadelphia, and across the Niagara River in Bridgeburg, Ontario, Canada. Known initially for its telephone communication products, it entered the wireless business in 1921 when it introduced its first complete receiver, the Federal Junior. At its peak the Federal factory in Buffalo operated 24-hours a day employing over 1,000 workers. In 1926, the company's name changed to the Federal Radio Corporation but faced increasing competition in the household consumer market from such companies as RCA, Westinghouse, Zenith, Crosley, and Emerson. Following the stock market crash in October 1929, Federal Radio ceased production.

WGR's first day of programming included an address and prayer by Rev. Michael Ahern, president of Canisius College; a concert by the Yankee Six Orchestra; a discussion on the growth of Buffalo business by Albert Kinsey, president of the chamber of commerce; and a presentation on the advantages of a college education by Dr. Julian Park, from the University of Buffalo. During the first year of operation, the broadcasting day only consisted of a few hours of programming each evening.

The following is from a published report in the *Buffalo Evening News* on May 22, 1922: "WGR is the highest-powered broadcasting station between Schenectady and Detroit and is said by radio experts to have by far the highest percentage of efficiently in the country. The station has been attractively arranged and furnished. The broadcasting room is hung with heavy gray drapes. These are not only pleasing to the eye but necessary to kill off any ring or echo that might interfere with the broadcasting as they improve the acoustics. There is an adjoining lounge and waiting room comfortably arranged with wicker furniture."

In 1923, WGR moved its studios and transmitter from its original location on the top floor of the Federal Telephone and Telegraph Company in North Buffalo to the newly opened Statler Hotel in downtown Buffalo located on Delaware Avenue at Niagara Square. In promotional materials, WGR billed itself as "the most powerful radio sending station in America."

HOTEL STATLER
AT BUFFALO

THE HOME OF WGR

WGR
Federal Telephone & Telegraph Company

Daily Broadcasting Schedule
Eastern Standard Time
319 Meters   940 Kilocycles

- 10:45 A. M.   *Weather forecast for Western New York and Buffalo.*
- 12:00 Noon   *Market, Produce and Live Stock Markets reports. Monday and Thursday—Agriograms.*
- 12:30 P. M.   *Organ Dining Room Hotel Statler George Albert Bouchard*
- 2:30 P. M.   *Orchestra Music.*
- 3:30 P. M.   *Closing Prices of N. Y. Stock Exchange*
- 4:30 P. M.   *Tea Time Music, Harp and Violin, Palm Room.*
- 6:30 P. M.   *Vincent Lopez, Hotel Statler Orchestra.*
- 7:30 P. M.   *Digest of the day's news. Second broadcasting of all daily reports. Tuesday—Scientific American Paper. Thursday—Boy Scout Radiograms, Industrial Employment Bulletin. The American Boy Story.*
- 9:00 P. M.   *Monday, Wednesday and Friday—Concert Program.*
- 11:00 P. M.   *Monday, Wednesday and Friday—Vincent Lopez, Hotel Statler Orchestra.*
- 3:00 P. M.   *Sunday—Vesper Service.*
- 4:00 P. M.   *Sunday—Organ, Robert Munn.*

No reports, except weather, on Saturday and Sunday.
Special broadcasting on short notice at odd hours, especially from conventions being held in the Hotel.
Details announced in leading papers.

Chickering Grand Piano installed by Goold Brothers

Here is WGR's programming schedule from 1923. With its studios and transmitter located inside Buffalo's most modern hotel, the station took advantage of the Statler's daily musical entertainment such as organ recitals from the ballroom or violin music played at the hotel's Palm Room.

Federal first operated experimental station 8XAD before receiving its commercial license in 1922. The station's initial 250-watt transmitter fit on two wooden kitchen tables, which had been bolted together. By 1924, with the transmitter now located at the Statler Hotel, WGR was operating on a frequency of 940 kilohertz and 500 watts. Technical advances quickly saw the transmitter's power increased to 1,000 watts in 1926.

Early live programming from Buffalo included the *Bing Family Show* sponsored by Bison Oil Products. In the publicity photograph, a mock "parlor" was created as the fictitious setting for the Bing family.

Pioneer broadcaster Herb Rice began his radio career in 1928. He spent 14 years at various stations, including WGR, WKBW, WBEN, and WMAK. As WGR's program director, Rice sought out top-notch local talent that included Robert Schmidt, who would eventually be known as "Buffalo" Bob Smith of *Howdy Doody* fame. Following his career in Buffalo, Rice worked for the National Broadcasting Company.

As a young boy, longtime Buffalo broadcaster Ed Tucholka started his radio career as a boy chorister on WGR. Even at an early age, Ed possessed a deep rich baritone voice that helped him land his first announcer job in the late 1930s at WEBR radio. Tucholka would work in Buffalo broadcasting until his retirement in 1995. He passed away a year later in 1996.

For almost 30 years, David Cheskin conducted the WGR staff orchestra and acted as the station's music director. A stable of talented Western New York musicians appeared daily on the station, and the Cheskin Orchestra was one of the most popular acts both on air and in area dance halls. In 1944, the Dave Cheskin Orchestra was featured on a national broadcast over the Columbia Broadcasting System (CBS). This 1940s-era image features announcer John Lascelles (far left), Cheskin (far right), and feature singer Elvera Ruppel at center.

One of the original superstars of Buffalo Radio in the 1920s and 1930s for the Buffalo Broadcasting Corporation on WGR and WKBW, Roger Baker was the Queen City's first definitive sportscaster. Calling Bison games in the 1930s from Offermann Stadium, he was straight and by the book. After being tapped by baseball commissioner Kenesaw Mountain Landis to call the 1933 World Series to a nationwide audience on CBS, Baker landed a job in Cincinnati calling the National League Reds on WLW. After the war, Baker returned to Buffalo and read the news on WKBW Radio but, eventually, moved into the general manager's office at the short-lived Buffalo UHF pioneer WBES-TV, where he also read the news. Along with Bill Mazer, Baker was also an original member of the WGR-TV sports team when the station signed-on in 1954. Baker moved to Albuquerque, New Mexico, for health reasons and continued his broadcast at KOB for several more years.

WGR's Billy Keaton gained fame in vaudeville before entering radio. He honed his witty and comedic timing on thousands of stages across the country before transforming his routine into the popular *Stuff and Nonsense* show on WGR. First starting as a temporary assignment, Billy was joined by his wife, Reggie, and the couple hosted the *Mr. and Mrs. Show* until the mid-1950s. The Keatons transitioned into Buffalo television in 1954 as pioneer personalities on WGR-TV. Billy Keaton passed away in 1976, and Reggie died in 1995. Both were inducted into the Buffalo Broadcasting Hall of Fame in 2005.

Between 1934 and 1936, *Rubinoff & his Violin* was a popular network program airing on WGR and sister station WKBW. This ad from the summer of 1935 also promotes Buffalo's "natural air-conditioning" due to its strategic geographic location on the shores of Lake Erie.

As an ever-increasing slate of network shows took over timeslots once filled by Buffalo talent, local news became an important part of WGR's programming day. Without a dedicated news staff of its own, WGR partnered with the large, local staff of the *Buffalo Times* newspaper to deliver headlines.

The outbreak of World War II catapulted radio's importance as a primary new source as wire and network services such as the Mutual Broadcasting System supplied "break news" from both the European and Pacific fronts. With a large map of the world behind them, two WGR broadcasters provide updates from the front window of a downtown Buffalo department store.

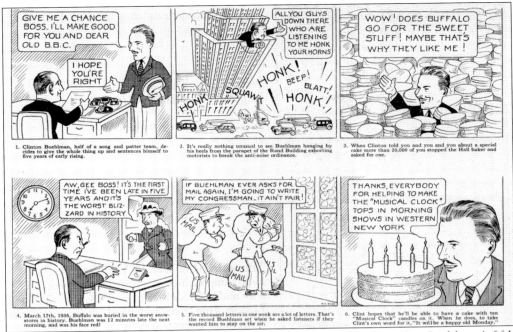

In 1936, WGR published a 24-page, commemorative booklet celebrating Clint Buehlman's fifth anniversary at the station and the success of his *Musical Clock* morning show. Proceeds from the public sale of the publication benefitted the American Red Cross of Buffalo. This cartoon summarized Buehlman's first years at the Buffalo Broadcasting Company that included causing traffic jams in Lafayette Square and receiving a record 5,000 letters in just one week.

In this staged photograph, sharply dressed men and women wait for their time to perform in the WGR reception area located on the 18th floor of the Rand Building in downtown Buffalo. WGR would officially move into this Art Deco–style skyscraper on May 1, 1929.

Officially opened in July 1941, the Buffalo Broadcasting Corporation constructed a new $350,000 transmitter and tower facility on Big Tree Road just south of the downtown core on Big Tree Road. Housed inside the Art Deco structure were the technical elements that put WGR and sister station WKBW on the air.

A technological marvel at the time of its construction, WGR would frequently provide public tours of the facility. Guests would have entered the transmitter building through the main door, walk up a stairwell lined with glass brick, and arrive at the visitors' gallery. The second floor housed two glass-enclosed control rooms, one for WGR and the other for WKBW. A stainless-steel railing separated visitors from a wall of transmitters covering three sides of the room. Tours only lasted a short time, as World War II security concerns ended the public's access to the transmitter site. As of 2021, both WGR and WKBW are still using the transmitter site with modern equipment.

The "Dean of Buffalo Sports Radio," sports broadcaster and journalist Ralph Hubbell joined WGR in 1939 where he provided play-by-play of all Bison baseball home games and recreated away games using Western Union messages. Hubbell began his radio career at WEBR in 1935 by reading poetry over the air but soon found that his fortune in sports. Over the years, "Hub," as he was known to friends and fans, was a man for all seasons as he did play-by-play for every major college and professional team in Buffalo.

Here, WGR's Ralph Hubbell throws a few punches with rival WBEN sports report Jim Wells at a banquet at the Statler Hotel. Hubbell would leave WGR in 1948 to join WBEN. He was inducted into the Buffalo Broadcasting Hall of Fame in 1997 and died in 2000.

Bill Mazer came to Buffalo in 1947 where he signed on as a sportscaster. One year later, he became sports director for WGR radio. Mazer dominated Buffalo sports radio serving as play-by-play man for all of the city's major sports, including both the Buffalo Bisons hockey and baseball teams, the All-American Football Conference Buffalo Bills, and Little 3 (Niagara University, St. Bonaventure University, and Canisius College) basketball. As a seasoned broadcaster fluent with years of play-by-play and commentary under his belt, Mazer left Buffalo for New York City in 1964.

Following the 1946 dissolving of the Buffalo Broadcasting Corporation, WGR separated from WKBW to become a standalone station. At the top of new station ownership and management were two pioneers of the radio industry who submitted a $750,000 bid to purchase the station. Leo Fitzpatrick was formally one of the principal owners of WJR, Detroit. I.R. Lounsberry was once the personal assistant to Dr. Lee DeForest and was partner and manager of WMAK in 1922. The duo would sell their interests in WGR in 1954.

Listeners tuning into WGR in 1954 would be welcomed by a personality lineup that included mornings with John "Old Bones" Lascelles, Billy Keaton in the afternoons, and Bob Glacy keeping the overnight shift entertained with his *Glacy's Basement* program.

There are many myths and legends surrounding the WGR call letters and if they have a meaning. Many believe the call letters were chosen to honor an early investor into the station, George Rand. Over the decades, the station also positioned itself as the "World's Greatest Radio," and in this print ad from the December 1953 issue of *Broadcasting* magazine, "Wherever you Go there's Radio!" The truth is that the Federal Telephone and Telegraph Company was randomly assigned the call letters WGR by the US Department of Commerce in 1922.

"Hold the Phone!" John Otto is considered the "Dean of Buffalo Talk Radio," having been a pioneering host of the format for over 40 years. Otto hosted evening chat sessions on WGR over two periods after spending five years in the 1980s at WKBW. His five-decade tenure in Buffalo radio, the majority of if at "55 on your dial," included the city's best-known talk shows *Extension 55* and *Night Call*. His last show took place on December 3, 1999, and he died a few days later on December 6, 1999, at the age of 70. Otto was inducted into the Buffalo Broadcasting Hall of Fame in 1989.

John Otto began his career in radio broadcasting on WBNY where he was a disc jockey and covered news. Always willing to fill any shift or try something new, he even read children's stories over the air as "Brother John Otto."

BROTHER JOHN OTTO - 8 a.m. SUNDAY

With the top of Buffalo Central Terminal seen just peaking behind, WGR's John Lascelles takes the throttle of a New York Central E8 diesel locomotive as a publicity stunt for a station promotion.

Danny Neaverth briefly joined WGR before heading across the dial to WKBW where he would become one of the Buffalo's most beloved and popular radio personalities for 26 years. In this image, Neaverth, holding the WGR sign, is joined by John Zach. A few years after this picture was taken, Zach would join Neaverth as his *Pulse-Beat News* man at KB.

Two of WGR's mobile news cruisers await fast-breaking action behind WGR's studios, located at 2077 Elmwood Avenue. The station would call a small building behind WBEN-TV's studios home for much of the 1960s.

Frank Benny joined WGR Radio in 1965 and undoubtedly was one of the station's most popular personalities for much of his 19 years there. In 1977, when Benny was afternoon host, the station won *Billboard* magazine's radio station of the year award. In addition to radio, Benny's talents would be utilized by sister television station WGR-TV as a sports and weather anchor as well as host of telethons, movie matinee programs, and as the station's primary voice talent. Benny died in 2005 and was inducted into the Buffalo Broadcasting Hall of Fame in 2010.

On March 30, 1969, WGR held one of the most memorable promotions in Buffalo broadcasting history. The Great WGR Easter Egg Drop had 10,000 plastic eggs filled with price coupons dropped from the WGR helicopter. The event took place over 10 Western New York parks and attracted tens of thousands of listeners. WGR's in-copter host for the stunt was Frank "Bunny" Benny. In total, 9,876 eggs were redeemed at Erie County Savings Bank in downtown Buffalo.

A 2004 inductee into the Buffalo Broadcasting Hall of Fame, longtime morning host Stan Roberts was known for his corny jokes and puns that would make Buffalo laugh and groan. Roberts was the morning personality on WKBW from 1963 to 1971 before leaving for Boston. He would join WGR a year later in 1972 where he held down the a.m. drive until 1982.

When Buffalo received a National Hockey League expansion franchise in 1970, a young Ted Darling was given the honors of becoming the team's first radio play-by-play announcer. As the original "Voice of the Buffalo Sabres," Darling spent 22 seasons and almost 800 games being with fans. His amazing career was cut short by Pick's Disease. He was inducted into the Buffalo Broadcasting Hall of Fame in 2002.

Pictured in February 1970, WGR Radio's Bell "Jet Ranger" helicopter cruises over downtown Buffalo providing morning and afternoon traffic reports. Just below the WGR logo on the aircraft is one of the station's legendary studio locations, the Art Deco Rand Building.

Pictured is WGR studios at 464 Franklin Street in Buffalo's Allentown District. The station would broadcast out of this building until consolidating facilities with sister station WWKB on Elmwood Avenue.

WGR's "Silver Bullet" mobile studio was a frequent attraction at the Erie County Fair where listeners could see live broadcasts as well as meet personalities like George Hamburger, Joe Galuski, Chuck Lakefield, and Tom Langmyer.

Shane Gibson first came to Buffalo in 1973 as part of WKBW's "Great America Talent Hunt" to replace fast-talking Jack Armstrong. Although he came in second place, his on-air persona "The Cosmic Cowboy" captivated Buffalo radio listeners and would allow him to join the station a few months later as the station's night personality. But it would be at WGR that "Shane Brother Shane" legend in Buffalo would flourish until 1985 and again for a brief stint in 1989. Gibson was inducted into the Buffalo Broadcasting Hall of Fame in 2011 and passed away in 2021.

The WGR Sports Department 1989 to 1993 consisted of (left to right) Greg Brown, Jeff Morrison, and Pete Weber. Brown was the Buffalo Bills radio color analyst from 1991 to 1993. He provided play-by-play for the Buffalo Bisons until 1993, when he joined Pittsburgh's KDKA radio to take over similar duties with the Pittsburgh Pirates. Having provided play-by-play for the Buffalo Bills, Buffalo Bisons and Buffalo Sabres, Weber joined the Nashville Predators during their inaugural year in 1998 to be their play-by-play voice.

Conservative talker Jay R. Gach joined WGR in 1991 to replace outgoing talk host Paul Lyle. In later years, Gash would team up with his wife, Suzie, to provide brash, edgy political and social commentary. Originally from Philadelphia, Gash came to Buffalo via Anchorage, Alaska. In 1993, Gash would leave Buffalo to accept a job in New Orleans.

At the height of the Buffalo Bills' American Football Conference Championship years, Chuck "The Coach" Dickerson was king of sports talk on WGR and hosted a three-hour afternoon, drive-time show. Dickerson, a Bills assistant from 1986 to 1991, was blunt, provocative, and loud. He would often end his show, after arguing with callers, with the catchphrase "Who love ya, baby?" Dickerson joined WGR in 1993 and departed 10 years later in 2003.

Tom Langmyer is one of the most respected industry consultants and managers in modern America radio. After receiving his FCC Third-Class license at the early age of 14, Langmyer would eventually work at Buffalo stations WGR, WBEN, WJJL learning all aspects of the broadcasting business including on air, promotions, engineering, and programming. After managing top market stations such as KMOX, St. Louis; WGN, Chicago and WTMJ, Milwaukee he founded a media acquisition and consulting company, Great Lakes Media Group, in 2018.

On the evening of his 1998 induction into the Buffalo Broadcasting Hall of Fame, WGR's John Otto broadcasted his program live from the site of the ceremony, Buffalo's Tralfamadore Music Hall. It was a truly a memorable night as countless Buffalo broadcasting legends paid homage to Otto behind a pair of vintage RCA microphones. WGR's operations director Jim Pastrick facilitated the historic broadcast with help of station engineers Dan Gurzynski and Matt Monin. Otto would pass away a year later in 1999.

Two
WEBR

In 1930s high style, band leader King Brady strikes a pose in front of a WEBR Western Electric 600a carbon microphone. Brady's orchestra was a popular feature on early radio broadcast and at ballrooms across Western New York.

The City of Buffalo's second "licensed" radio station, WEBR, signed on the airwaves on October 14, 1924. Owned by Herbert H. Howell's Howell Electric Company, the station was located inside the company's building at the corner of Niagara and Franklin Streets. Given sequentially issued call letters, Howell adopted the slogan "We Extend Buffalo's Regards."

May 8, 1945, was "Victory in Europe Day" as the Allied Forces officially defeated Germany in World War II. WEBR provided wall-to-wall coverage of the events with both local reaction and unprecedented reports from across Europe via the Mutual Broadcasting Network. The celebrations would be brief, as the war in the Pacific would last for another year.

WEBR and its staff enjoyed several "firsts" and triumphs. Among them were the adventure stories written by program director Fran Striker in the late 1920s. He developed stories with a western theme and sold the scripts to other radio stations across the country. The hero in his story—the Lone Ranger.

In 1936, the station was sold to the *Buffalo Evening News* and became affiliated with the Blue Network of the National Broadcasting Company (NBC). A host of network stars, including Dinah Shore, Walter Winchell, Jack Armstrong, and "The Quiz Kids," was featured on WEBR's program schedule. Six years later, in 1942, *Buffalo Evening News* sold WEBR to competitor *Buffalo Courier-Express*.

In 1944, WEBR became an affiliate of the Mutual Broadcasting System. After the war, WEBR changed dial position from 1340 to 970 AM.

WEBR's longtime home was located in a converted Victorian-era mansion at 25 North Street in the city of Buffalo. "Broadcasting House," as it was known, housed offices, studios, the record library, and performance spaces. The station would occupy the building until 1993, when it moved to Buffalo's waterfront to studios at Horizons Plaza, home to Western New York Public Television.

WEBR's mobile van, known as the "Squirt Caravan," could be found across Western New York attending store openings, groundbreaking ceremonies, parades, and so on. WEBR's aggressive promotions department and its affiliation with the *Buffalo Courier-Express* newspaper provided the station with a competitive edge over stations with larger power and better dial positioning.

Children growing up in postwar Buffalo undoubtedly listened to *Hi-Teen* with host Bob Wells. The show, believed to be the model for Dick Clark's *American Bandstand*, was the epitome of the clean-cut, saddle-shoed white Anglo-Saxon 1950s. No rock and roll here, only guest appearances by the likes of Perry Como, Frank Sinatra, Les Paul, and Mary Ford.

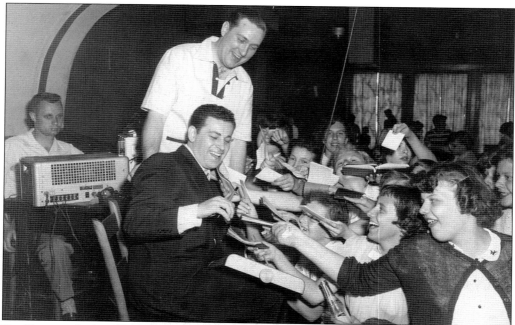

For 17 years, the live *Hi-Teen* broadcasts originated from the Dellwood Ballroom, located at the corner of Main and Utica Streets in Buffalo. In this image, Bob Wells looks over the shoulder of Julius La Rosa as he signs autographs for a mob of *Hi-Teen* attendees.

Pictured in 1948, two lucky teens receive their *Hi-Teen* prizes from WEBR promotions director Bill Schweitzer and Bob Wells during a *Hi-Teen* broadcast from the Elks Club on Delaware Avenue. Bob Wells was inducted into the Buffalo Broadcasting Hall of Fame in 1997.

Bob Wells interviews actor and producer Franchot Tone in 1951 to promote the film *Here Comes the Groom*. Tone was a native of Niagara Falls and was a leading man appearing in MGM, Universal, and Paramount pictures during the 1930s through the 1950s.

Bob Wells is surrounded by an entire stage filled with prizes consisting of Niagara Falls–made Nabisco Shredded Wheat. Bob Wells was one of the first inductees into the Buffalo Broadcasting Hall of Fame in 1997; he passed away in 1989.

Pictured is the inside the WEBR transmitter building located on Cloverbank Road in the town of Hamburg. From here, the station's signal was received from "Broadcasting House," located at 23 North Street in the city.

Here is an architectural rendering of the WEBR transmitter facility, located south of downtown Buffalo. The antenna array behind the building drove a powerful, but pencil-thin, 970 signal, straight to the north, through the city of Buffalo, Niagara Falls, and Toronto.

Dan McBride was a journeyman broadcaster who was a part of Western New York's radio scene for over 60 years. McBride first caught the broadcasting bug while hanging out at the Babcock Street Boys Club with Danny Neaverth, Bill Masters, and Joey Reynolds. It was there that the four boys began their own in-house "radio station," playing records for dances, the club's game room, and before and after basketball games. In 1959, McBride joined WEBR as assistant promotions manager and fill-in announcer. Danny was well known across Buffalo through his work as an assistant and cohost with Bob Wells and Ed Little at sock hop dances. McBride passed away in 2016.

On October 2, 1948, the *Billboard* Magazine recognized WEBR's *Hi-Teen* as the top-rated record show in Buffalo. With a signal reaching the Toronto metro area, WEBR did extremely well with national commercial sponsors and advertisers.

Here, WEBR's news cruiser and mobile studio posed in front of Broadcasting House at 23 North Street.

WEBR's Jack Eno and Carrol Hardy "Extend Buffalo Regards" with a tip of the hat during the station's "sing-along" era in the mid-1960s.

During the early 1960s, as other Buffalo stations turned to more lucrative formats such as Top 40, WEBR doubled down on a format geared towards mature adults. *Sing-Along Radio* put the spotlight on "Tin Pan Alley" American standards of the 1920s and 1930s. Song booklets were distributed across the region to encourage housewives to let loose with their singing talents.

WEBR format became the "Sound of the City" during the mid-1960s based on a series of jingles sung by the famous Johnny Mann Singers. So popular were the jingles that a 45-rpm record was produced for the public.

Pictured on August 10, 1957, Town Casino owner Harry Altman is interviewed by WEBR's Lucky Pierre. The occasion was a live broadcast and benefit at the "Town" to raise money for a young Eggertsville boy who was electrocuted by a 2,400-volt power line.

Ed Tucholka, center, was known for his breezy manner and for being one of the best ad-libbers in the business. He credited his ability to talk on the fly back to the days when he manned the public address system at Buffalo's famous Sattler's 998 Broadway Buffalo department store. In 1941, he started his *Noonday Review* on WEBR and grew the show to having one of the biggest listening audiences in Buffalo. In this image, Tucholka teams up with Lucky Pierre to interview Liberace.

Ed Little spent a breathtaking 62 years on radio, nearly all of it in Buffalo and Rochester. That career took root in 1938 when he stepped in front of a microphone at WEBR as a child actor with a grownup voice. During World War II, Little carried a wire recorder aboard B-29 bombing missions over Japan and delivered the play-by-play description for playback on NBC Radio. Joining WEBR postwar as a music personality, he soon became host of the late-night Town Casino broadcasts, interviewing every megastar of the 1950s from Danny Thomas, pictured here in 1953, to Tony Bennett, Johnny Ray, and Rosemary Clooney.

Here is an early 1960s WEBR 970 Record Hop Club membership card featuring personalities Danny McBride and Ed Little. The duo would make the rounds to almost every school gymnasium in Buffalo, spinning records, hosting dance contests, and serving up samples of sponsor-provided Pepsi-Cola. After a long career that included being an on-air personality and station manager at WBNY FM, McBride started his own advertising agency, which he operated until the late 1990s.

In 1961, the WEBR traffic copter cruises over downtown Buffalo and the entrance to the Sky Way Bridge. In 1993, the area just below the copter would become the new home to 970am with the opening of Western New York Public Broadcasting Association's Horizons Plaza broadcasting center.

WEBR's Jack Sharpe became Buffalo's first traffic copter reporter when he took to the skies on April 29, 1959. Flying with a Western New York–built Bell 47G-2 helicopter, Sharpe became famous for his frank and honest descriptions of what was going on beneath him. Sharpe parlayed his broadcasting career into a successful run in politics, eventually becoming the supervisor of the Town of Amherst.

Jack Eno epitomizes the soother elegance and friendly spirit of WEBR across nearly four decades at the station. A crackerjack personality quizmaster, newsman, drama director, and program chief, he was one of Buffalo broadcasting's most versatile performers and managers. Straight out of college, Eno started in 1935 as WEBR's "Olde Town Crier" and still was working daily at the station until 1975, when he died at age 62. He was posthumously inducted into the Western New York Broadcasting Hall of Fame in 1999. This is Eno at the mic in 1959 when, as WEBR midday man, he interviewed the legendary Les Paul and Mary Ford with Buffalo mayor Frank Sedita.

From 1961 to 1964, "Big Al" Meltzer was a member of the WEBR stable of talent, hosting the station's morning show as well as handling sports duties. He left Western New York for Philadelphia where he spent 50 years covering sports and handling play-by-play duties for the 76ers, Eagles, Phillies, and Big 5 basketball. Meltzer died at the age of 89 on June 12, 2018.

In 1975, the Western New York Public Broadcasting Associating purchased WEBR, and a year later, it transformed the station into the country's first public all-news radio station. Broadcasting veteran Jack Mahl, left, was hired to bring his decades' worth of experience into the newsroom filled with young, intelligent, and eager journalists like John Martin, center, and Mary Jo Malone, right. The station's coverage of the Blizzard of 1977 won accolades from listeners and from industry professional as its aggressive news gathering forced commercial stations in Buffalo to increase their coverage and staffing.

In November 1976, WEBR Newsradio 970 station manager Bill Devine and promotions manager Jim Wenzel accept the donation of a new Buick Skyhawk to act as the station's official news cruiser. As a public broadcasting station, WEBR received a tremendous amount of community financial support to fuel its innovated, all-news format. Thirteen hours a day, there was a constant flow of copy in the newsroom, located at 23 North Street, being pumped out by a news staff that was mainly between the ages of 21 and 28. In addition to managing 970 AM, Devine also directed the operations of WEBR's sister station, all-classical WNED FM.

While attending Buffalo State College in the late 1960s, Al Wallack landed a job at WKBW and began a 40-year career in broadcasting. After stints at Washington, DC's WPGC and Buffalo's WWOL, Wallack joined WEBR AM as the all-night man in 1972, moving to middays and then to the position of production director. In 1976, when the station was sold to Western New York Public Broadcasting, Al stayed on to create *Jazz in the Nighttime*, a popular show which he hosted for the next 18 years. When the format of the station changed and jazz was discontinued, Al became operations director for WNED AM and FM.

In 1983, Al Wallack was part of team that recreated an episode of Fran Striker's *Covered Wagon Days*. Written in 1930, this show was the precursor of the Lone Ranger. Al is seen here playing the part of the "Foley artist," creating sound effects just like it was done in the 1930s. Other members of the cast included Laurie Githens, Mark Hamrick, Dave Waples, and Dennis Keefe.

In 1978, WEBR became the nation's top-rated public radio station. From the 1970s through the early 1990s, a full-service news department was staffed by the likes of Jerry Fedell, Kevin Gordon, Leon Thomas, Jack Mahl, Scott Brown, John Gill, Mike St. Peter, Mike Allen, Teresa Beaton, and Jim Ranney. Dave Kerner, Sam Anson, and Pete Weber made up the core of the WEBR sports department.

In the early 1990s, following federal government funding cutbacks for public broadcasting stations, WEBR's local news operations were substantially streamlined, and its call letters were changed to WNED AM. In 1993, the Western New York Public Broadcasting Association consolidated its radio and television station into one building on the Buffalo waterfront, leaving 42 North Street silent without a radio station for the first time since 1935. In July 2014, a storm severely damaged the building, causing the City of Buffalo to issue an emergency demolition order.

Three
WBEN

This image of a WBEN quartet exemplifies the youthful energy that was radio in the 1930s. Pictured are, from left to right, soprano Sylvia Brimmer, pianist Karl Koch, alto Evelyn Hager, and vocalist and pianist Loretta Clemens. Karl Koch, center, was staff pianist for WBEN starting in 1930. Koch began playing piano at age 10, and by the time he was 15, he was playing background music for silent movies. He had the honor of playing "The Star-Spangled Banner" on WBEN Radio's inaugural broadcast on September 9, 1930. In 1933, Clemens would join the NBC Network with her banjo-playing brother Jack. The duo presented their talents to a national audience several times a week. Loretta would also play a role on the NBC's show the *Gibson Family*.

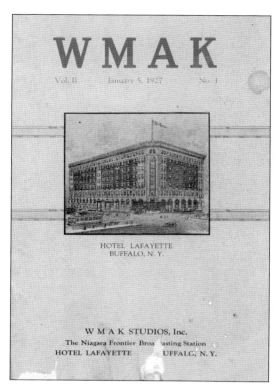

The ornate Hotel Lafayette opened its doors in 1904. The building's large ballroom and strategic location in downtown Buffalo made it a favorable location for radio and television stations during the history of Buffalo broadcasting. WMAK, a precursors station to WBEN, began broadcasting from the Hotel Lafayette in 1925.

One of the biggest acts to come out of WMAK and early Buffalo radio was the comedic duo of Stoopnagle and Budd. Wilbur "Budd" Hulick and Frederick Chase "Stoopnagle" Taylor came together in 1930 as a team unexpectedly when they were called to duty to fill airtime during a station technical failure. What resulted was a barrage of spontaneous, impromptu comedic patter that had local audience demanding more. A year later in 1931, the team was signed to broadcast nightly, except Fridays, over the Columbia Broadcasting System.

Posed on a piano inside the Statler Hotel studios of WBEN is an on-air quartet made up of Robert Butler, Karl Koch, Loretta Clemens, and Tony Pecore.

During the 1930s and 1940s, WBEN's popular dramatic programming featured the area's best actors as well as worthy offerings from skilled Western New York writers. Pictured behind the scenes of *King's Castle* in 1932, members of the cast of a mystery dramatic production over WBEN gather around the microphone for rehearsal. The program aired Sundays at 7:00 p.m. Standing are, from left to right, George Otto Ward as Charlie King, and Anne Smart, as Loki Douglas, the two leading characters. Also pictured are Martha Hawkins, Ethel Hinton, William Steinell, Charme Allen, and Albert H. Zink. Seated at left are director Harold Fair and author Lloyd Graham.

From February 6, 1932, the WBEN *Dinner Timers* provided "sparkling melodies" to entertain listeners during the dinner hour each day at 6:05 p.m. From left to right are (standing) Robert Butler, tenor; Sylvia Brimmer, soprano; a quartet composed of Malcolm C. Brock, first tenor; Sidney F. Brown, second tenor; Percy G. Chatwin, bass, and William Poole, baritone; Jack Clemens, guitarist; and Tony Pecore, violinist; (sitting) Karl Koch and Loretta Clemens, pianists.

Programming on WBEN began at 9:00 a.m. on Tuesday, September 9, 1930, with the formal opening of its studios on the 18th floor of the Statler Hotel the evening before from its main studio. It operated at 900 kilocycle at a wavelength of 333.1 meters. The *Buffalo Evening News*, owners of the station, reported that "men and women in evening dress crowded the reception room and offices in the Statler" in anticipation of the inaugural broadcast. Merwin Morrison had the distinction of being the first voice heard on the station.

In a control room that was located between studios, WBEN technicians would gaze over the control board and operate various microphone. In this view from the mid-1930s, engineers oversee a broadcast by a vocal trio and accompanist.

Studio B of WBEN, which was attractively finished in green, terra-cotta, and white, was devoted principally to individual performers and small groups.

To learn about radio and modern technology, Buffalo schoolchildren were frequently guests of WBEN for field trips and live performances. In this staged photograph, children learn about the job of a sound effects specialist, known as a "Foley man."

Robert Emil Schmidt grew up on Buffalo's Eastside and attended the former Fosdick-Masten Park High School, now City Honor. While in school, he formed a singing trio with two other students, Johnnie Eisenberger and Elmer Hattenberger. His show business career was sparked when singer Kate Smith happened to hear the young singers on a program, sponsored by Simon Pure Beer. An ultra-talented performer, Schmidt possessed a quick wit, a powerful singing voice, improvisational piano skills, and good looks. As his popularity increased, Schmidt began using the stage name Bob Smith.

In 1946, Smith left WBEN to join NBC in New York City. People started call him "Buffalo" Bob, and the nickname stuck. One of his duties was hosting a children's Saturday quiz program called *The Triple B Ranch* with Big Brother Bob. In a 1983 interview, Smith said, "I had this little Mortimer Snerdish country-bumpkin character. He was originally called Elmer. He'd come out and say, 'Uh-huh-huh, Howdy Doody, kids!' So the kids naturally started calling him that." When NBC started television broadcasting, Smith talked his bosses into a children's show on NBC-TV, which debuted December 27, 1947. He called it *Puppet Playhouse* at first, then the *Howdy Doody Show*.

As a staff pianist at WBEN, Bob Smith teamed with Clint Buehlman on a morning audience-participation show, and he also hosted a midday program that include songs, chatter, piano, and recorded music. Smith was inducted into the Buffalo Broadcasting Hall of Fame in 1998.

WBEN's broadcasting team from the mid-1960s included, from left to right, (first row) Van Miller, Stan Barron, Jack Ogilvie, and John Luther; (second row) Bill Masters, John Corbett, Clint Buehlman, Ken Philips, Gene Kelly, and Al Fox.

WBEN's Mildford "Joe" Wesp was known as the "Ironic Reporter." He joined the station in 1930 and gained fame visiting and reporting from unique locations across the region and focusing on human interest stories. Formally a newspaper journalist, Wesp was a decorated World War I veteran who was honored with the Gold Cross of the Order of Merit of Poland. During the early 1950s, Wesp hosted the station's six-days-a-week farm show featuring livestock prices, news, music, and Joe's pungent brand of homespun philosophy. The Household Finance Corp. sponsored his programs for over 20 years. Wesp, who later joined WBEN-TV as its daytime news editor, passed away on October 2, 1960, at age 60.

From 1942 until his brief tenure was interrupted by military service in 1943, Jack Paar was host of WBEN's morning program, *The Sun Greeters Club*. The show had limited success as it struggled to gain an audience against Clint Buehlman's *Musical Clock* on WGR. While in Buffalo, Paar challenged management by using his lightning-fast humor to make on-air fun of client's commercials. In part to his fast comedic quips, Paar choose not to return to Buffalo following the war as his talents were discovered by the national networks. In 1957, Paar was chosen to succeed Steve Allen as host of NBC's *Tonight Show*, a position he held until 1962.

For a generation of Buffalo radio listeners, Clint Buehlman was morning radio in Buffalo. "Yours truly, Buehly," as he called himself on air, was on WBEN from 1943 until his retirement in 1977. His program was known for its mix of news, music, and commentary with the occasional joke. He became the "voice of school closings" during Buffalo winters. One of Clint's more popular features was the checking of outside temperatures by referring to "Arthur Mometer."

Comedian Bob Hope jokes with WBEN's Clint Buehlman inside the station's Statler Hotel studios. Buehlman was hired away from WGR after the departure of Jack Paar.

Not only did Buehlman develop a strong relationship with his listeners, but also with his sponsors who purchased his program by the quarter hour. Many of the sponsors were personal friends of Clint who received his personal endorsement for services and products. Many of his sponsors continued to support his programs on WGR and WBEN for more than 40 years.

After Buehlman aired his final show on July 29, 1977, WBEN listeners flooded the station with requests for his return. Although not on the air daily, his voice was continued to be heard on commercials, and he returned to do a series of Sunday morning shows in 1979. Buehlman passed away in 1997 at the age of 85.

Norm Wullen performed as WBEN's staff organist for 30 years. His music was featured on morning breakfast shows originating from the Statler Hotel and later from AM&A's department store's Yankee Doodle Room. He started at WBEN radio in 1934 and appeared during the early days of WBEN-TV, starting in 1948. When organ music on radio began to lose popularity, Wullen continued to share his talents as the organist for the Buffalo Sabres from 1970 until 1985. He passed away at the age of 99 in 2004.

Ralph Hubbell was already an established radio star when WBEN brought him on board from WGR in 1948. At WBEN, Hubbell would take over the duties of radio sports director and also pioneer local sports on television when WBEN-TV sign on the air in May 1948.

In 1966, after 18 years at WBEN and more than 30 years total on Buffalo airwaves, Ralph Hubbell resigned from the station for health reasons. His time away from the microphone lasted only 28 months, as he was back doing a daily sports show on WGR radio. He would continue to work on various radio and television projects while "retired" up until his death in 2000.

By his own counting, Buffalo native Jack Mindy worked for 28 radio station across the country during his 50-year career in broadcasting. His longest stint was from 1978 to 1987 where his friendly, cheerful voice was heard as afternoon host on WBEN. He was born with radio in his blood, as his father was an early radio pioneer in the 1930s at WEBR. Mindy's Buffalo station stops also included time at WYSL, WGR, and WWKB. Mindy retired from radio in 2009 and passed away on March 8, 2022.

WBEN staff consisted of Harry Webb, Ralph Hubbell, Don Cunningham, James Gardner, and Robert Redden.

On November 16, 1956, Arthur Godfrey originated his coast-to-coast CBS radio broadcast via WBEN from the Wheatfield plant of Bell Aircraft. An accomplished pilot, Godfrey landed his own private DC-3 airplane, arriving just 75 seconds from his scheduled broadcast. The 90-minute program originated from the private office of Leston Faneuf, president and general manager of Bell Aircraft, where they talked about Bell's development of the X-2, guided missiles, and groundbreaking helicopters.

In January 1960, WBEN moved from the 18th floor of the Statler Hotel to its new home at 2077 Elmwood Avenue. The building was original constructed by NBC for its short-lived UHF television WBUF, Channel 17 in 1956. In this image, keyboard artist Norm Wullen, host Mike Mearian, chief announcer Carl Erickson, and newscaster Jack Ogilvie test out the acoustics of "Studio B." WBEN would call North Buffalo its home until 2000, when owners Sinclair Broadcasting moved its radio facilities to Amherst.

An integral part to the success of Clint Buehlman was his right-hand man behind the scenes, Tom Whalen. Whalen was Buehlman's studio engineer from 1947 until Clint's retirement in 1977. Whalen first got into radio as a ham operator in 1938 and then became a part of the Army's Air Corps communication staff during World War II. Following the war, Whalen joined WBEN and retired in 1983 after 36 years of service.

Lou Douglas joined WBEN radio in 1957 and was a continued presence inside the station's newsroom until 1987. As a crack radio journalist, he covered many of the biggest news events in Buffalo including the Blizzard of 1977 and the 1971 Attica prison uprising. Douglas passed away in 2017.

Before gaining fame on Buffalo television with the "Weather Outside" and as "Commander Tom," Tom Jolls was a member of the WBEN staff. Jolls arrived at WBEN in 1962 from WUSJ, Lockport, where he hosted a variety of programs until his departure to WKBW-TV in 1965. In this image, Jolls, lower right, is directing fellow WBEN staff members Ward Fenton, Bill Peters, Martha Torge, and Mike Mearian.

WBEN's Van Miller, Stan Barron, and Dick Rifenburg handled the broadcast duties for both University of Buffalo and Buffalo Bill football on WBEN. Rifenburg played college football for the University of Michigan Wolverines in 1944 and from 1946 to 1948 and played professionally in the National Football League (NFL) with the Detroit Lions for one season in 1950.

The "Voice of the Buffalo Bills" for 40 years, WBEN's Van Miller is regarded as one of the greatest professional football announcers of all times. Miller received his start in radio at WFCB in Dunkirk in 1950 and would join WBEN as a summer replacement announcer in 1955. From that day on, he stayed at WBEN radio and television for 43 years, never missing a day's work and turning down offers from NBC, CBS, and ABC to remain close to his family in Dunkirk. Miller would retire from broadcasting in 1998.

The *Van Miller Show* was an early-afternoon favorite of men and women alike. Van featured items of interest from homemaking tips to the latest on bowling or fishing. This, coupled with celebrity interviews, light humor, and good music, made the show extremely popular.

This staged photograph inside the press box at War Memorial Stadium featured sitting at center, from left to right, Van Miller, Stan Barron, and Dick Rifenburg, along with an army of spotters and statistician who supported the broadcast of Buffalo Bills football.

In 1965, Stan Barron moved from WKBW to WBEN to work in the station's growing sports department. Until 1984, Barron hosted the station's evening sports talk show call, *Free Form Sports*. Barron used his influence in sports to help orchestrate the return of minor league baseball to Buffalo in 1979. Barron died in 1984.

In 1981, Buffalo Sabres head coach Scotty Bowman, seated right, is seen in WBEN's Studio A with Stan Barron.

In the 1980s, WBEN was able to secure the broadcast rights for the Buffalo Sabres and assembled an all-star crew to provide play-by-play. The team included Rick Jeanneret, Ted Darling, Mike Robitaille, and Jim Lorentz. After 51 years associated with the Sabres radio and television broadcasts, Jeanneret retired from the microphone in 2022.

Voice of the Buffalo Bills John Murphy hosted WBEN's *One on One Sports* from 1984 to 1992 and continued the tradition of sports reporting excellence at the station. He has been associated with Buffalo football as a color analyst from 1984 to 1998. In 1998, he took over play-by-play duties from the retiring Van Miller.

Tim Wenger (left) with former WBEN personality and sales executive Stan Roberts. From the newsroom to management, Wenger has been behind many of WBEN's biggest successes during the 1990s and 2000s. He first joined the station in 1986 as a full-time assistant to the program director and part-time news anchor. In 1988, he took over the station's traffic copter duties, then became the evening news anchor. In the early 90s, Wenger was named WBEN's news director followed by program director and in 2000 was named operations manager for Entercom's WBEN, WGR and WWKB station cluster. In 2021, he was named the news/talk format vice president for Audacy stations nationwide while continuing to lead Buffalo operations. His broadcasting leadership mantra is, "great talent + great content = ratings & revenue."

Here is an inside look at WBEN's master controls, with Dick Rifenburg at the helm, following the 1974 modernization of WBEN studios. The massive Ward Beck control board stayed in use until 2000, when the station moved to a new location in the Buffalo suburb of Amherst.

Part of being an "all-service" radio station were daily farm reports from WBEN's Al Fox. The WBEN *Farm Report Show* premiered in 1947 and aired for 28 years.

In 1988, WBEN was one of the first station in the country to add the syndicated *Rush Limbaugh Show* to its lineup. Rush's popularity was credited for saving many AM radio stations and building a new audience of mainly politically conservative listeners. Limbaugh passed away on February 17, 2021. By May 2021, WBEN would replace the Limbaugh program with a local show hosted by David Bellavia and Tom Bauerle. In this picture, Limbaugh jokes around with Sandy Beach inside the station's 2077 Elmwood studios.

Bill Lacy first arrived at WBEN in 1980 to host the late morning shift and took over WBEN's morning show in 1984. For 16 years, he would carry on the WBEN tradition of providing a warm and friendly voice in the morning with music, weather, traffic, and of course, winter weather school closings. In the mid-1990s, when the station switched format to all news and talk, Lacy was joined by Kevin Keenan. Lacy was part of the WBEN family until 2000. In 2001, he was hired by WHTT-FM, where he spent 21 years hosting the morning show before retiring in 2022.

Originally joining WBEN as a staff announcer in 1948, Ed Little's 62-year radio career would take him to stations in San Diego and Rochester before rejoining WBEN in 1981. His classic, authoritative voice was a hallmark of WBEN's service for 20 years. Little would have the distinction of being the last live voice to broadcast from WBEN's home at 2077 Elmwood Avenue in 2000. Ed was inducted into the Buffalo Broadcasting Hall of Fame in 2000; he passed away in 2001. Former WEBR personality and WKBW *Pulse-Beat News* announcer Ed Little joined WBEN in 1981 after spending 14 years at WBBF in Rochester. His trademark delivery added distention to that station's aura until his retirement in 2000.

At the time of his death in 1993, Jim McLaughlin was considered "Buffalo's foremost radio news director." McLaughlin joined WBEN following the station's purchase by Larry Levite's Algonquin Broadcasting. His Buffalo radio resume included stops at WYSL and WBEN where he was credited by being the first to hire a female news staff member, the first to dedicate a full-time streets report, and the first to use shortwave radio to monitor developing breaking international news. In 1979, he won an Associated Press award for the "Best Regularly Scheduled Radio News Program" for his *Newsday at Noon* block of programming. Poor health forced McLaughlin to retire from radio in 1987.

In 1978, Jeff Kaye would replace WBEN's Clint Buehlman as morning host. "People are frantic in the morning and it's my responsibility to get them in a good mood so they think well of me, of WBEN and our clients," said Kaye. "I do it by being a warm human being on air."

Kaye would depart WBEN and Western New York in 1984 to become one of the principal voices for NFL films. Kaye died on November 16, 2012, at age 75.

In 1978, Larry Levite formed Algonquin Broadcasting and with a group of local investors bought WBEN from the *Buffalo Evening News*'s owners Berkshire Hathaway. Levite began his broadcasting career as a sales executive in 1967 at WYSL/WPHD and quickly advanced to general manager. He would join WEBR as general manager and infuse new, creative energy into the aging station. Under Levite's creative leadership, WBEN was able to compete with ratings-dominant FM stations by retaining and hiring some of the best broadcasters in Buffalo. He would own WBEN until the mid-1990s. Levite, a member of the Buffalo Broadcasting Hall of Fame, passed away in 2017.

Some people are just born to be journalists. Such is the story of WBEN's Brian Meyer, who started his own neighborhood newspaper while in the fifth grade. Following his graduation for Marquette University, Meyer would join WBEN in 1982 as a street reporter. For over 15 years, he was the station's go-to man at city hall to cover breaking news and to travel out of Western New York to bring national stories back to Buffalo. Meyer would leave WBEN in 1997 to join the *Buffalo News*. More importantly, he has been the media mentor to hundreds of journalists through his teaching career at area universities and with his legendary internship program.

For a self-proclaimed "non-broadcaster," Tom Bauerle has had an incredible four-decade run on Buffalo radio. Lauded for his "leadership and character" at graduation from Kenmore West High School, Bauerle was still a student when he was recruited to work at WJJL, Niagara Falls. In 1982, WGR news director Don Dussias heard Tom and hired him for part-time news work and Sabres coverage at WGR 550. At the early age of 19, he was given the opportunity to take over John Otto's Extension 55 evening program following Otto's move to WKBW. In 1991, Bauerle took over mornings on WGR, where his *Breakfast with Bauerle* consistently provided the station with strong ratings. Citing ABC's Peter Jennings and WKBW's Irv Weinstein as career influences, Tom's calm and insightful coverage of 9-11 shined the spotlight on his journalistic background. Shortly after the tragedy, he moved over to WBEN, where he has been station's marquee personality ever since. Bauerle's journalistic professionalism and on-air compassion was again called into action during WBEN's breaking news coverage of the racially motivated supermarket mass shooting that took place on May 14, 2022.

For almost four decades, Randy Bushover has been a key behind-the-scenes contributor to WBEN's continued success. He has performed virtually every job inside the station's control room, including ground control traffic, board operations, phone screening, production work and show producing. Not limited to "off air" work, Bushover has cohosted Sports Sunday, is the voice of WBEN's daily business segments, and is host of the station's Sunday morning show. Bushover's experience and leadership has brought him professional accolades during breaking news events such as the 2006 "October Surprise" storm or the 2009 crash of Colgan Air Flight 2407 in Clarence, New York.

Four

WKBW

One of the most colorful, successful, and controversial pioneers of Buffalo radio broadcasting was Dr. Clinton Churchill. He was one of the first religious leaders in America to discover the power of mass communication. In his twenties, as a vice president of his father's insurance company, Churchill found his religious calling during a 1917 revival conducted by Billy Sunday where he publicly accepted Christ into his life. Following his conversion, Churchill proclaimed his testimony to congregations across Western New York and began to amass a large following. In 1918, he began his formal religious education, and in 1920, he organized the Churchill Evangelistic Association. On April 12, 1925, the home for the congregation, the Churchill Evangelistic Tabernacle, opened at 1420 Main Street. That year, Churchill became a pioneer of religious broadcasting in America when he began using radio to bring his sermons to the masses. This was his first taste of the influence that radio could have over his mass audience as thousands of letters, many containing money, began pouring into the station's mailbox. In 1926, Churchill acquired a one-kilowatt Western Electric transmitter and applied for a broadcast station license. On October 15, 1926, the Churchill station was granted sequentially issued call letters WKBW and its authority to operate. On Wednesday, October 20, 1926, WKBW was granted its first license and went on the air with Buffalo's "first commercially-built radio transmitter." Dr. Churchill would pass away in 1973 having sold the station to Capital Cities Broadcasting in 1961.

THE CHURCHILL TABERNACLE, BUFFALO'S LARGEST SPIRITUAL WORKSHOP

During its initial weeks of broadcasting, WKBW's transmitter was located inside the Churchill Evangelistic Tabernacle near Main Street and Utica. This caused issues with neighboring radio listeners as the station was causing a great deal of interference on its 1,380-kilocycle channel. After being reprimanded by government regulators, technicians focused this signal, and service returned to normal. Most early programming consisted of religious services from the Tabernacle with Dr. Churchill at the microphone.

On November 7, 1926, an official dedication ceremony for radio station WKBW took place inside the Churchill Evangelistic Tabernacle. In addition to religious hymns and blessings, Dr. Churchill provided the prayer of dedication. At this time, the station began using its air slogan that incorporated its call letters, "Well Known Bible Witness." Churchill originally requested the call letters 'WAY" in keeping with the religious intention of his mission, but those call letters were on a ship in the marine radio service.

In September 1929, WKBW's licensee name was changed from the Churchill Evangelistic Association to WKBW, Inc., and it began commercial operations. It was at this time that WKBW joined forces with WGR, WKEN, and WMAK to form the Buffalo Broadcasting Corporation (BBC). Operations were consolidated, and the BBC moved into the 18th floor of the recently constructed Rand Building. The 24-story structure at Broadway and Washington Street faced Lafayette Square. At this time, the BBC owned or controlled four of Buffalo's six operating station.

The Rand Building's location in Lafayette Square made it easy for hosts to conduct live "man on the street" interviews with passersby. Frequently, broadcasters will wave from the 18th floor to listeners below to illicit approval of shows and entertainers. At this time, studios were maintained at both the Rand Building and in the Churchill Tabernacle on Main Street.

Located 10 miles south of Buffalo on a rise of land not far from the shores of Lake Erie, the Buffalo Broadcasting Company, operators of WKBW, officially opened its new $350,000 transmitter and tower facility in 1941. The Art Deco structure housed WKBW's powerful, 50,000-watt transmitter. Four 350-foot antenna towers were able to send KB's signal in an area covering 13 states and Canada.

Direct telephone lines carried WKBW's programs from the Rand Building to the transmitting station located on Big Tree Road in Hamburg. In the transmitter control room, radio engineers constantly check the tone, quality, and volume of the programs. Employees were responsible for 200 dials and a myriad of signal lights that monitored the flow of power and the function of the complex electrical equipment to stay in accordance with Federal Communications Commission (FCC) regulations.

From left to right, WKBW's Larry Brownell, Foster Brooks, Al Anscombe, and chief engineer Leroy Fidler are seen during a live broadcast from Buffalo's Memorial Auditorium. Brooks spent some of his formative years in Buffalo before moving to the national stage. While at the Buffalo Broadcasting Corporation (WGR/WKBW), he hosted a program called *The Musical Clock* and later WKBW's *Million Dollar Ballroom*. Brooks passed away in 2001. Al Anscombe began his career as a junior sports announcer in the late 1930s before rising to vice president and station manager at WKBW.

In an industry heavily dominated by men, Helen Neville was among the first to break the barriers that got in the way of women in broadcasting. Her remote broadcasts from downtown department store became extremely popular with tens of thousands of listeners. After WKBW, Neville would join WGR radio and then became part of the inaugural staff of WGR-TV in 1954. She was inducted into the Buffalo Broadcasting Hall of Fame in 1997.

In 1947, Wilbur "Budd" Hulick and his wife, Helen, joined WKBW to present a popular "husband and wife–style" show. Hulick was one of Buffalo's earliest radio stars, having gained fame as part of the Stoopnagle-and-Budd duo with Frederick Chase Taylor. In this image, Bud and Helen interview and another husband-and-wife duo, Jamestown native Lucille Ball and Desi Arnaz, during a promotional visit to Western New York.

In 1929, WKBW affiliated with the "Columbia Chain." It then began sharing CBS programming with Buffalo's WMAK, the original Buffalo-area Columbia affiliate. From the building's 18th floor, WKBW frequently provided programming, such as orchestra music, to a national audience through its affiliation with the Columbia Broadcasting Company.

In 1942, a new FCC policy would limit owners to one radio station in each market, and the BBC's monopoly of WGR and WKBW was challenged. The breakup of the two entities proved to be a complicated, litigious process to unravel as Churchill signed a 99-year lease for WKBW with the BBC in 1931. In 1947, Churchill took back sole ownership of WKBW from the BBC and began looking for a new home for its studios. In 1948, it signed a long-term lease for 12,000 square feet of space on the 10th floor of the Victor Building on Genesee Street. Six large studios were planned with room to grow to a potential television station. This plan for a great broadcasting facility in downtown Buffalo was eventually canceled in favor of retrofitting an aging carriage house next door to the Churchill Tabernacle on Main Street.

Buffalo architect Melvin Morris proposed a modern facade for the former Churchill carriage house, featuring gleaming white tile and an artistic representation of the "Spirit of the Airwaves" to proclaim, "Buffalo's Most Powerful Station." The actual improvements to the building's exterior included the faux, cantilevered accents and large WKBW sign, but it did not include the mural as depicted in the rendering.

On October 25, 1950, WKBW's studios moved from the 13th floor of the Rand Building to a new, modern "Radio Center" office and building at 1430 Main Street. The station occupied the same property where roughly 25 years earlier WKBW first went on the air with the first commercially built transmitter ever used in Buffalo. With a signal ten times more powerful than any of Buffalo station, programming from this small building would blanket the Eastern Seaboard from Maine to North Carolina.

Behind the updated facade of WKBW's building at 1430 Main Street could be found small, but technically modern studios sufficient for disc jockeys, personalities and engineers to produce the station's local programming. Affiliation with the ABC network was dropped on June 1, 1956, and on January 2, 1957, the station briefly joined the NBC network.

One of the benefits of being located on Main Street was the ability to be seen by thousands of daily commuters. To take advantage of its location, and to have a gimmick to become relevant with morning listeners, WKBW debuted the *Clock Watcher* program in 1952, hosted by Dave Prince. Each morning between 7:30 a.m. and 9:00 a.m., drivers became indoctrinated to seeing Dave sitting underneath a big umbrella in front of the station in every weather condition possible. He would ask for "three toots for good luck" and encourage people to join his "Aren't You Glad It's Friday" club. In October 1952, Pat Fagan replaced Prince as the "Clock Watcher," who had left Buffalo for the West Coast.

Primarily known for his work calling the play-by-play for Buffalo Bisons baseball and the All-American Conference Buffalo Bills, Bill Mazer could also be heard hosting a four-hour music show on WKBW called *Mazer's Matinee*. Debuting in 1950 and billed as "Buffalo's Biggest Afternoon Program," the show featured phone requests for Western music in the first hour and requests for popular music for the remaining time.

While at WKBW, Bill Mazer not only solidified his reputation as one of Buffalo's premier sports reporters, but also hosted talk and music shows. In this 1950 image, Mazer takes part in a parade down Broadway past the famous "998 Broadway" location of the legendary Buffalo department store Sattler's.

After leaving WKBW to join WGR radio and television, Mazur would pack up for New York City in 1964 where he enjoyed a nearly 40-year run as a sports broadcaster.

On July 10, 1960, Roger Baker delivers a 15-minute world and local news roundup from the front window of Sattler's department store, located at 998 Broadway.

Stan Barron, center, joined WKBW in 1952 and was a jack of all trades at the station. Barron could be heard heading up sports-by-play, hosting music programs, and waving to Main Street drivers during a stint as WKBW's "Clock Watcher." In this image, Stan is joined by (left to right) Clint D. Churchill, promotions manager, station general manager Al Anscombe, Polish programming host and radio sales manager Stan Jasinski, and salesmen Jim McGrath and Roger Baker.

Stan Jasinski was the "Voice of Buffalo's Polish American Community" during an unprecedented 60-year career in radio. A native of Detroit, Michigan, Jasinski's accomplishments included success on air, in radio sales, and eventually, as a station owner. Using his experience in sales and management, he started his own station, WMMJ, in 1964, and he later led a group of investors to found WUTV Channel 29 in 1970. Stan was still immensely popular up until his retirement in 2000 at the age of 85.

Stan "Stas" Jasinski reached one of North America's largest Polish American communities centered in Buffalo with a variety of programs on WKBW. In 1953, Jasinski could be heard daily on *Polka Beehive*, Saturdays on the *Polka Party*, and on his *Sunday Polish-American* program, which featured news and commentary in the Polish language. Stan was honored by the Buffalo Broadcasting Pioneers in 1997 and passed away in 2005.

An American radio pioneer and Buffalo's "Father of Rock & Roll Radio," George Lorenz began playing rhythm and blues record in the mid-1940s on WXRA and moved to WJJL Niagara Falls in 1948. Only in his late 20s at the time, his deep voice made him sound older, and he soon gained the nickname "Ol' Man Lorenz." At WJJL, he was given the freedom to play what he wanted and soon added rhythm, blues, and even country music to his show. Between 1953 and 1955, Lorenz left Western New York for Cleveland where he crossed paths with disc jockey Alan Freed; however, he longed to be back in his hometown of Buffalo. In 1955, he joined WKBW where his style of rock and roll radio could be heard over KB's 50,000 signal.

Lorenz became came known as "Hound Dog" or the "Hound" in 1951. The nickname had its roots in a 1940s expression "doggin' around." In 1971, Lorenz told the *Buffalo Evening News*, "One of the jive expressions at the time was if you were hangin' around the corner, you were doggin' around. So I'd come on and say, 'Here I am to dog around for another hour.' That's how they got to call me the hound dog." (Image from the Collection of Betty Shampoe).

A savvy marketer, Lorenz founded the "Hound Dog" fan club that was made up of thousands of teenaged members from across the Eastern Seaboard. In addition to membership card, the Hound published a month newsletter called the "Hound Dog's Howl."

George Lorenz would call WKBW home until July 1958, when the station would switch to a Top 40 format. The Hound left the station because of "creative freedom," as he felt Top 40 radio would decrease the chances of a new artist getting his or her music to be played. Lorenz passed away on May 29, 1972.

On July 4, 1958, a seismic shift in Buffalo radio took place that would change the medium forever. WKBW switched its format and heralded the arrival of "FutureSonic Radio," the catchphrase given to WKBW to its brand new, fast-paced, imaginative music-news-service operation. Soon to be gone was KB's ethnic, country and western, and religious programming, as well as George Lorenz, who would not conform to a strict Top 40–style playlist.

Under the guidance of Dick Lawrence, director of programming, promotions, and publicity for the station, KB made a drastic change in its format by virtually eliminated all previously carried programs, both network and local, and substituting what Lawrence called, "ultra-modern broadcasting techniques designed to entertain, inform and serve the greatest majority of the radio audience." The Even Newer WKBW was "formula radio," which meant a meticulously planned and programmed 24 hours per day of popular music, strong disc jockey personalities, up-to-the-second news and sports flashes, and public service features.

The first true Top 40 format in Buffalo was inaugurated in the summer of 1957 at WBNY AM. The mastermind of the format was program director Dick Lawrence. Lawrence came to Buffalo with almost 14 years of broadcasting experience under his belt in May 1957, from Omaha, Nebraska, where he was news director of Todd Storz's KOWH. As program director of WBNY, he shot the 250-watter from near obscurity into first place on both the Pulse and Hooper surveys. WKBW Station manager Al Anscombe had been studying the modern trends in broadcasting as markets across the country felt the power of the Top 40 format. WBNY's success was enough to convince Anscombe to hire Dick Lawrence away from the small station. (Courtesy of Bob and Terry Skurzewski.)

Tom Shannon began his broadcasting career at WXRA, now WUFO, at the age of 15 doing everything at the station from staff announcing to landscaping. With movie star good looks and an ultracool demeanor, Shannon was bound to be one of the first teen idols of Buffalo broadcasting. In 1958, he was hired at WKBW as a newsman and, eventually, given the opportunity to be a weekend and fill-in jock. Little did he know that, later that year, the station would flip format, become "FutureSonic Radio," and create a legend. He was not the wise guy or the funny guy on radio, but the epitome of youthful coolness. So popular was Shannon's theme song, "Wild Weekend," that it would be recorded by the Rockin' Rebels and become a No. 8 hit on the Billboard charts. In 1963, Shannon moved down the dial to WGR AM but soon departed for CKLW in Detroit. Shannon returned to WKBW in 1983 but was let go after an ownership change in 1986. He would return to his hometown, this time to the FM dial at WHTT in the 1990s and retired from the station in 2005.

JIM TAYLOR   TED HACKETT   TOM SHANNON   DON KELLER   DICK BRAUN   GENE NELSON   BOB DIAMOND   RUSS SYRACUSE

WKBW's all-star personality lineup of 1961 included Jim Taylor, Ted Hackett, Tom Shannon, Don Keller, Dick Braun, Gene Nelson, Bob Diamond, and morning man Russ Syracuse. In 1962, WKBW owner Clinton D. Churchill purchased KYA in San Francisco. Churchill offered a number of KB jocks the opportunity to transfer to the new station. Soon, popular WKBW personalities Russ Syracuse, Gene Nelson, Doug James, and Tom Saunders headed to the West Coast "KB" at KYA.

This WKBW lineup was nothing to sneeze at. Seated inside a giant tissue box during a marketing promotion are, from left to right, Don Keller (Yearke), Tom Shannon, Doug James, Wayne Stitt, Jay Nelson, Russ "The Moose" Syracuse, Danny Neaverth, and Tommy Saunders.

Rochester native Irv Weinstein joined WKBW Radio in 1958 to become news director of the station's *Pulse-Beat News* department. The news at 15 and 45 minutes past each hour, and Irv's edgy writing, fast-paced reading, alliteration, and tabloid story selection made the news sound as exciting as the Top 40 records being played.

In 1964, Irv Weinstein would move to WKBW-TV as the station's lead anchor, a position he would hold until 1998, when he would retire as the most popular television personality in the history of Western New York broadcasting. He was inducted into the Buffalo Broadcasting Hall of Fame in 1998 and passed away in 2017.

Jim Fagan was part of WKBW's news team for more than three decades. As a member of the station's *Pulse-Beat News* starting in 1960, Fagan's authoritative voice cut through the disc jockey patter and Top 40 records to deliver headlines of the day. He was a constant on the station until the station became automated in 1988 but returned the following year when KB adopted a business news format. When the news department was again abolished in 1992, he returned in 1993 to cohost a labor-oriented news program. Fagan was inducted into the Buffalo Broadcasting Hall of Fame in 2002 and died in 2016.

Stan Roberts replaced WKBW morning man Jay Nelson in 1963 to begin a seven-year run as KB's morning mayor. Roberts would leave Buffalo for a stint in Boston before returning to Western New York in 1972, joining WGR AM.

Danny Neaverth is one of the longest-working and most beloved personalities in Buffalo radio history. His interest in radio began as a teenager at the Babcock Street Boys Club in 1951 where, alongside friends Danny McBride, Bill Masters, and Joey Reynolds, he would spin records on a closed-circuit radio station. Neaverth honed his professional radio career at WFRM, Coudersport, and WDOE, Dunkirk, before joining WBNY radio. From 1961 to 1986, Neaverth was an ever-present force at KB, propelling ratings at every turn. His playful humor made him a star during afternoon drive time and "cross-over" with pal Joey Reynolds shortly before 7:00 p.m. was must-listen-to radio.

In 1962, Danny Neaverth is "locked up" outside a sponsor location during a spoof of the movie *Birdman of Alcatraz*. Neaverth would work afternoons at KB until October 1970, when he took over the KB morning show.

On March 15, 1965, Danny Neaverth was mobbed by fans for his autograph during a WKBW live remote. Always a "ham," Neaverth took pride in his "boy next door" persona and was always willing to be the focus of self-deprecating, "straight man" humor. He is a member of both the Buffalo Broadcasting and New York State Broadcasters Association Halls of Fame.

Dr. Churchill singed on WKBW television in 1958 with a studio located next door to the station. The relationship between to the two stations allowed many KB personalities the opportunity to host their own television shows. In 1960, Danny Neaverth is a guest on *Buffalo Bandstand*, hosted by fellow WKBW disc jockey Tommy Shannon.

With his lightning-fast wit, South Buffalo's Joey Reynolds quickly became one of WKBW's all-time biggest personalities. His nightly show was heard across the Northeast over KB's 50,000 signal and showed up in ratings in faraway markets, such as New York City.

In 1961, WKBW, Inc., owned by Dr. Clinton Churchill, sold to WKBW radio and television to Capital Cities Broadcasting for $14 million in cash. The new ownership doubled down on promotions and the hiring of talented broadcasters, including Joey Reynolds.

Disc jockeys, including Joey Reynolds, would find additional sources of income by hosting sock hops or promoting their own concerts. This is a poster for Joey Reynolds's concert featuring the Gentrys and the Kingsmen.

Royal Order of the Night People

This certifies that

Jim Moyer

is a loyal member of the
WKBW ROYAL ORDER OF THE NIGHT PEOPLE
the world's most exclusive organization.
This card is NEVER to be shown to a non-member.

SERIAL NUMBER

N⁰ 25118   A

Joey Reynolds
exalted leader

At the end of each show, Reynolds would "induct" listeners into his Royal Order of the Night People (RONP) Club, asking them to pledge allegiance to his show and KB. RONP membership cards, like this, became cherished keepsakes for thousands of teenagers.

Fred Klestine's radio career began by accident when he took cover from a passing rainstorm inside a Delaware Avenue bar and met the general manager of WWOL. When hearing Fred's deep, rich voice, the manager invited him to audition. After WWOL, Klestine would join WNY in the late 1950s before jumping to WKBW in 1961. A memorable career highlight was the night that 10,000 KB fans turned out to Memorial Auditorium to see Klestine and fellow KB jock Joey Reynolds wrestle the professional team of the Gallagher brothers. Klestine left WKBW in 1971 and worked at various Buffalo radio stations until 1991. He passed away in 1992.

Rod Roddy spent five years at Buffalo WKBW AM in the 1960s and, fondly, once told the *Buffalo News*, "Those were my drinking days. There are more bars and churches in Buffalo than any other place." After a successful career in radio, Roddy found newfound fame as the announcer for CBS's *The Price Is Right*. Roddy passed away in 2003.

WKBW's 1966 lineup of VIPS included Jefferson Kaye, Fred Klestine, Danny Neaverth, Rod Roddy, Stan Roberts, and Lee Vogel.

One of the most creative minds to ever work in Buffalo radio, Jeff Kaye joined WKBW in 1966, following the departure of Joey Reynolds. Originally hired to fill the evening timeslot, Kaye's talents would shine as KB's program director, where he put together and managed one of the most successful radio lineups in the history of modern radio. His expert writing and production skills resulted in his 1968 and 1971 localized adaptations of Orson Welles's *War of the Worlds*.

This group of radio outlaws stemmed the tide of cookie-cutter programming that started to dominate American radio in the early 1970s. With FM's influence gaining fast and most AM music stations opting for "more music" formats, personality-radio seemed headed for the proverbial last roundup. In 1972, WKBW program director Jeff Kaye featured one of the greatest jock lineups in the history of Top 40 radio. From left to right are Casey Piotrowski, Jack Sheridan, Don Berns, Bob McRae, Sandy Beach, Jack Armstrong, and Dan Neaverth.

"Somebody call up those other guys and tell them to turn it [their station] off, they're running up their electric bill!" If there was anybody with more energy on the air, the world has yet to hear them. "Your Leeeeeader!!!!" Jackson Armstrong was the consummate screamer who rocked the Buffalo airwaves from 1970 to 1973 on WBEN. KB was Armstrong's 10th stop in a broadcasting journey that would take him to about two dozen North American radio station.

Another personality brought to Buffalo by KB program director Jeff Kaye was Don Burns. Burns joined WKBW's powerhouse lineup in 1970 and left for WPHD/WYSL in 1974.

Don Burns, pictured here with the Osmond brothers, would make the rounds at such legendary stations as WDRC, Hartford; KLIF, Dallas; WTAE, Pittsburgh; and pioneer alternative station CFNY in Toronto. In the early 1990s, Burns promoted Toronto's emerging electronic music community and was dubbed "Dr. Trance," as he helped to create the city's legendary rave scene. Burns passed away in 2016.

Sandy Beach joined WKBW via WDRC, Harford, in 1968. Within six years, according to a 1972 interview, program director Jeff Kaye was quoted saying that Sandy had "worked every shift on KB except *Morning Drive* and improved the rating in each part." His quick wit and infectious laugh were a part of Western New York until his retirement in 2020.

Sandy Beach would leave WKBW in 1974 to become program director at WJET in Erie, Pennsylvania. In the 1980s, Beach returned to WKBW before jumping to the FM dial in 1986; there, he would lead ratings at Hot 104 WNYS and then Magic 102 WMJQ. In 1997, he joined WBEN radio where he ruled talk radio in Buffalo until 2020.

Following the departure of Jackson Armstrong, KB program director Jeff Kaye held a national contest to find a replacement. In 1974, the *Great American Talent Hunt* featured top talent vying for the coveted evening timeslot. One of the participants was Ronald Maxwell Gibson, known as Shane. Shane ended up as the runner-up, but when the winner quit after only a few days, he was hired. Known as the "Cosmic Cowboy" and "Shane Brother Shane," he was a bigger-than-life personality who drove around in a flashy race car, wore pants with his name down the leg in sequins, and would frequently philosophize with deep thoughts about life on his show. Gibson was inducted into the Buffalo Broadcasters Hall of Fame in 2011, he passed away in 2021.

Rochester native Russ "The Moose" Syracuse was part of WKBW's original 1958 "FutureSonic Radio" collection of on-air personalities. He served in the Korean War and worked as a schoolteacher before beginning his radio career in Syracuse, New York. During his time at KB, he held down the late morning and midday shifts. In 1962, WKBW owner Clint Churchill offered Syracuse a transfer to his co-owned KYA in San Francisco. Syracuse died April 18, 2000. (Courtesy of Tom Syracuse.)

A new stadium brought a new era of Buffalo Bills broadcasting. In this scene from the first game played in Orchard Park's Rich Stadium on August 17, 1973, WKBW's Buffalo Bills broadcast team consisted of former player Ed Rutkowski, producer Jeff Kaye, play-by-play voice Al Melzer, and color commentator Rick Azar. (Photograph by Robert L. Smith.)

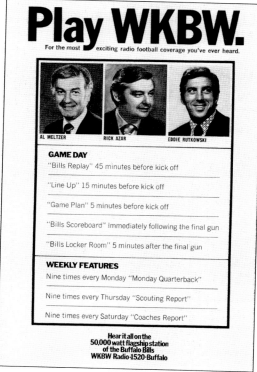

"Every party needs a brass band Mr. Wilson, WKBW will be your brass band." With those words from a contract proposal to team owner Ralph Wilson, WKBW pirated away the rights to Buffalo Bills radio broadcasts in 1972, leaving WBEN as odd-man-out for the first time since the days of leather helmets. Under the production leadership of program chief Jeff Kaye, KB revolutionized the way football was experienced on radio. The station presented expanded pregame coverage, elongated postgame coverage, a slam-bang "Buffalo Bills Replay," and a heavy emphasis on locker-room interviews. Many of Jeff Kaye's innovations went on to become commonplace nationally, and Kaye himself later became the official voice of *NFL Films*.

Jon Summers and station engineer Tom Atkins are seen inside the Buffalo Raceway Grandstand during a live remote from Erie County Fair. In October 1978, WKBW radio would move from its famous Main Street location to new facilities in Buffalo's Allentown district, located at 695 Delaware Avenue.

Although KB would lose ratings to emerging FM stations, Dan Neaverth remained as Buffalo's top morning man through much of the 1970s and 1980s. Holding down the afternoon slot in the late 1970s was Jay Fredricks. Fredricks, also known as Fritz Coleman, left Buffalo for Los Angeles in 1980 to work as a stand-up comic. In 1982, he joined KNBC-TV as a weekend weatherman and became the weekday weatherman in 1984. After a 39-year career at KNBC, Coleman retired in 2020.

Danny Neaverth
6:00 — 10:00 a.m.
KB radio 1520
Dan Kelley
2:00 — 7:00 p.m.

In 1985, WKBW owners Capital Cities announced an agreement to acquire the ABC television network. This merger would necessitate the sale of WKBW Radio because of a Capital Cities shareholder's involvement with the *Buffalo News*. On January 3, 1986, it was sold to Price Communications and formally ended its relationship with sister television WKBW-TV. With the sale saw a change of call letters to WWKB and a series of cost-cutting moves that included the firing of Tommy Shannon in February and the departure of Sandy Beach, who was replaced by Dan Kelley.

It was an end of an era in 1987. After 26 years at WKBW, it was announced that Danny Neaverth would leave the station that he was synonymous with for WHTT FM. A three-year, six-figure contract would see Neaverth replacing the departing Sandy Beach. The move would also allow Neaverth to be reunited with his son Dan Neaverth Jr., who was a sportscaster at WHTT, as well as work with his son Darren, who was involved in station sales. Neaverth Jr., pictured with his dad, first joined WKBW on air in 1983. Neaverth Sr. would work at WHTT until 2002, when his contract expired and was not renewed. In 2003, Neaverth would once again return to 1520 on the dial as Entercom Radio debuted a "KB Classic Format," complete with classic jingles and the return of legendary personalities, including a syndicated Joey Reynolds and Jack Armstrong. Unfortunately, the retro radio experiment on the AM dial ended in 2006 in favor of a switch to a talk format.

Five

TINY TOTS OF THE KILOWATT

WKEN signed on in 1927 by the Kenmore Presbyterian Church at Delaware and Hazeltine Avenues in Kenmore. In 1928, its transmitter and transmitter building, pictured here, were floated across the Niagara River by barge from Tonawanda to Grand Island. The *Buffalo Evening News* would eventually purchase the rights to the frequency, and the call would fade away into history.

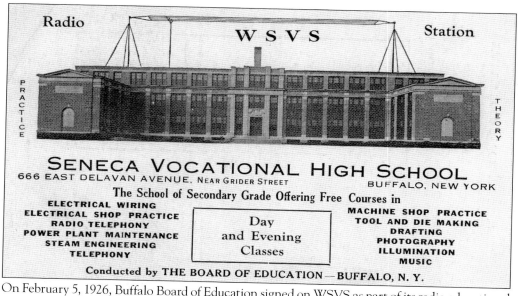

On February 5, 1926, Buffalo Board of Education signed on WSVS as part of its radio educational programs at Seneca Vocational High School, becoming the first vocational public school in the country to be granted its own broadcasting license. Using experimental equipment, principal Elmer Pierce is credited for bringing radio technology to the school as early as 1921, as he was an ardent and enthusiastic advocate of radio instruction. The station featured student-generated programming and encouraged students to learn the technical side to radio.

The *Fr. Justin Rosary Hour*, founded on Buffalo's Eastside, was one of the longest-running Polish language programs in American radio history. The show had its beginnings in 1926 as part of a Polish variety program, sponsored by the Kolipinski Brothers Furniture Company. Being religious people, the Kolipinski brothers wanted a spiritual dimension added to their weekly broadcast. Fr. Justin Figas, a Franciscan at Corpus Christi Church, was soon invited to deliver a five-minute message each week. The popularity of the segment soon eclipsed the variety program, and a year later, it became its own hourlong program. The *Rosary Hour* became a network program in 1931 when it was carried a across six stations. By 1954, the number of stations increased to 50 and reached 72 at the time of Father Justin's death in 1959.

One of the famed *Pulse-Beat News* men of WKBW, Henry Brach began his career at WBNY. As news director, he was the first person to hire Dan Neaverth as an announcer. In addition to news, Brach also hosted music programming at WBNY and WYSL FM before joining Irv Weinstein's staff at WKBW. Brach died in 1983 and was inducted into the Western New York Broadcasting Hall of Fame in 2002.

Before gaining fame on WKBW, "Daffy" Dan Neaverth was part of the pioneering Top 40 staff of WBNY Radio in 1957. Neaverth would leave WBNY for WKBW not knowing that program director Dick Lawrence would also leave for KB in 1958. Neaverth's initial move away from WBNY infuriated Lawrence so much that he immediately fired Neaverth when he took over KB to transform the station into "FutureSonic Radio."

WBNY went on the air on March 4, 1936, by Roy L. Albertson. At that time, it was assigned to a "shared frequency" with WSVS AM. Before switching format to Top 40, the station aired an eclectic mixture of ethnic programming and variety shows that reflected a wide audience of the city. The station remained a nonfactor in the market for decades until it adopted a Top 40 format under the direction of Dick Lawrence. The station would briefly have success until giant WKBW decided to do the same format bigger and better on its 50,000-watt signal. One of the early stars on WBNY was a young Kemal Amin Kasem, known on air as Casey Kasem. Kasem spent a year at the station in 1960 with his high-energy *Casey at the Mic* show. Following Buffalo, he found success at a number of West Coast stations and as a film and voice actor. In 1970, Casey would find international fame as host of the syndicated *American Top 40* countdown show.

Lucky Pierre Gonneau was born in France in 1934 and came to the United States at the age of 17 to attend Ithaca College for its Department of Theatre Arts. A born entertainer, his Buffalo radio career took him to WWOL, WHLD, WEBR, and WBNY. Following Buffalo, in 1955, he joined WOR, New York, before moving to Los Angeles to join KHJ-TV. At WBNY, Pierre enjoyed a rapid rise to popularity as a result of his rare combination of old-world charm and modern effervescence. Gonneau passed away in 2019.

WHLD, licensed to Niagara Falls, signed on in 1941 under the ownership of Earl Hull. The station call letters were derived from the initials of Hall's second wife, Hilda Lewis Hull. The station serviced the Falls with local news and content and was a proving ground for up-and-coming broadcasters like Lou Schriver and George Lorenz.

Earl C. Hull was a radio pioneer who entered St. Lawrence University in 1916 with impressive knowledge of wireless technology, which he later applied to communication problems on the battlefield. His talents helped put the university radio station on air in 1922. He built WKY in Oklahoma City (the United States' third commercial radio station). In 1940, he returned to Niagara Falls to establish WHLD.

Pictured are WHLD personalities Ramblin' Lou Schriver, Lucky Pierre (with microphone), and Rick Azar (wearing knit cap) during a radio remote. Azar later joined WKBW-TV as the station's sports director, where he would gain legendary status until his retirement in 1997.

Joe Rico is the most influential broadcaster and promoter of jazz music in Buffalo history. As a broadcaster, his radio shows in the 1950s introduced Buffalo jazz listeners to the best music jazz had to offer. He produced, coproduced, and promoted some of the greatest Buffalo jazz concerts of his time. His creative programming of jazz started at WWOL in 1949, then expanded to WHLD, WEBR, WGR, and WUFO. His smooth style, deep voice, and dedication to jazz earmarked him as the epitome of cool. Rico passed away in 2020. (Courtesy of Chris Podosek.)

Jack Horohoe began his radio career in the early 1960s on WNIA. With a deep, resonant voice, he worked at WBLK and then found himself doing middays at WEBR in 1968. In 1973, he left broadcasting to get into real estate but stayed active in the industry performing commercial work and as an active member of the Buffalo Broadcasting Pioneers. In 2020, when new owners of WJJL changed the call letters to WEBR, Jack was asked to return to radio 49 years later to recreate the feel of the "Sound of City." He passed away in 2020.

Barry Lillis was born and raised in Niagara Falls and started his radio career at WGGO in Salamanca, New York, in 1963. Lillis worked his way around the station across the country, finding his way back to Niagara Falls and WJJL 1440 AM. In 2020, he found himself back at 1440 AM, hosting music programming on the station. WJJL, licensed to Niagara Falls, signed on broadcast in 1947 with call letters standing for John J. Laux, its original owner.

The *Lockport Union Sun and Journal* newspaper signed on WUSJ AM from modern, art deco studios in 1949. The Corson family of Lockport owned the station until 1970 when it was sold to Hall Communication. The sale was necessary due to an FCC ruling that disallowed newspapers from owning print media and broadcasting stations in the same market. No longer affiliated with the newspaper, the call letters were changed to WLVL, meaning "Love Lockport."

WXRA 1080 AM, located in the small Buffalo suburb of Kenmore, was founded in 1948 by Thaddeus Podbielniak and Edwin R. Sanders. Originally using the call letters WNYB at the time of its construction permit, the station signed on in January 1948 with the call letters WXRA. In 1952, the city of license changed from Kenmore to Buffalo. Like most small-powered stations, WXRA offered a wide range of recorded programming, local news, and ethnic variety shows.

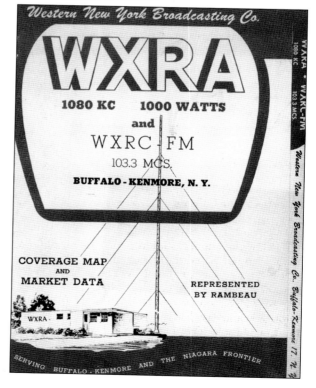

In 1957, Podbielniak and Sanders sold WXRA to John W. Kluge, who would go on to found Metromedia (owners of WNEW-TV in New York City). Kluge changed the station's calls to WINE and debuted a Top 40 music format on 1080 AM on October 15, 1957. WINE's city of license was changed from Buffalo to Amherst in 1959.

Here is the WINE "People's Choice" top song chart from Saturday, May 2, 1959. The station's Top 40 format at 1080am was short lived, as Dallas broadcaster and radio programmer Gordon McLendon purchased the station and changed it to "beautiful music" WYSL in 1960. Not finding immediate ratings success, McLendon moved the WYSL call letters and easy listening music to 1400am and sold 1080am to Leonard Walk in 1961. Following the sale, 1080am would be known as pioneer African American station WUFO.

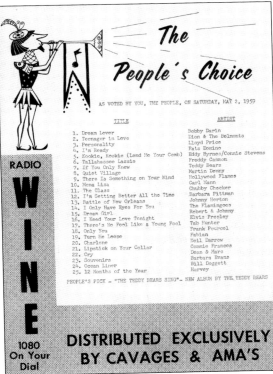

Station WWOL began its broadcasting on September 21, 1947, first operating from studios located in the Masonic Building on Ridge Road in Lackawanna. Its tower and transmitter were located off Abbott Road near the Buffalo city line. A year later, in 1948, the station moved into a modern studio located above the busy Shelton Square in downtown Buffalo, where, for many years, its billboard promoted the station as having "Better Programs, Better Reception, Better Results."

WWOL was founded by Leon Wyszatycki of Detroit, Michigan. Wyszatycki studied law at the University of Detroit and studied music at the Milan Conservatory in Italy. At one time, he had his own stock company that toured across North America. In 1930, he broke into Detroit radio, producing Polish language programs. In November 1946, Wyszatycki formed the Greater Erie Broadcasting Company with the express purpose of building a radio station in Lackawanna.

One of the first steps made in the direction of giving the Niagara Frontier something new in radio was the inauguration of foreign language programs. WWOL was the first radio station in Buffalo to provide listeners will a daily schedule of Polish, Italian, German, and Slavic programs. This image features a live radio broadcast promoting new polka recordings available from Ruda's Record Store at 998 Broadway. (Courtesy of Dennis Ruda.)

Stan Jasinski joined WWOL as its general manager at the station's inception in 1947. Jasinski began his career in 1930 at WEXL in Royal Oak, Michigan, and met WWOL founder Leon Wyszatycki while working at WJBK, Detroit. In addition to his managerial duties, Jasinski produced Polish language programs, skits, and special events, including live polka music broadcasts. So good was Jasinski's mastery of the Polish language that this American-born broadcaster was often taken for a native Pole for having acquired a fluent Warsaw accent. (Courtesy of Dennis Ruda.)

With 20 years of broadcasting experience behind him, Italian broadcaster Emelino Rico moved his programming to WWOL. *Casa Rico* aired Monday to Saturday from 11:00 a.m. to 12:00 p.m. and on Sundays from 11:45 a.m. to 1:00 p.m., reaching an Italian American population of 100,000 in the Niagara Frontier.

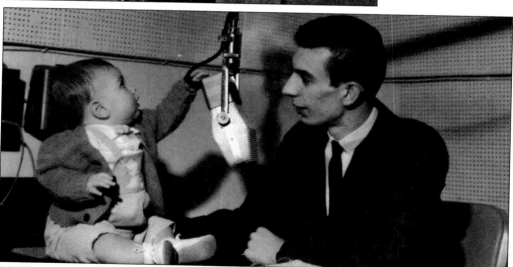

John Zach logged more than 60 years in Buffalo radio, primarily delivering the news in his own unique authoritative style. Originally hoping to be a rock and roll radio disc jockey, in September 1961, he found himself joining the WKBW *Pulse-Beat News* team, where he stayed until the news department was dismantled in 1988. His career reporting on the top news stories of the day would take him to WGR before joining WBEN in 1998, where he was part of an award-winning, morning show team that included cohost Susan Rose. After 18 years, Zach retired from WBEN in 2016 and then found himself drawn back to radio in 2017, this time at 1230 AM, WECK. He was inducted into the Buffalo Broadcasting Hall of Fame in 2002. (Courtesy of John Zach.)

Gerhard Keso produced WWOL's German programming that aired daily at 5:00 p.m. It was said that students studying the German language at the University of Buffalo would be directed to listen to his broadcasts to learn correct pronunciation and diction.

On July 3, 1955, WWOL became the site of a memorable radio prank that helped to signal a cultural shift at the beginning of the rock and roll era in Buffalo. The stunt involved disc jockey Tom Clay, who went by the radio name "Guy King." During his show, Clay climbed out of the window and climbed atop WWOL's billboard above Shelton Square. While on his perch, he solicited a response from listeners and passersby asking them to blow their horns while he repeatedly played "Rock around the Clock" by Bill Haley and the Comets. Clay's antics caused such a traffic jam in an already busy downtown Buffalo that police were called and the fire department was used to bring the young broadcaster down. Clay was charged with disorderly conduct and released into the custody of WWOL's owner.

Jimmy Lyons   Eddie O'Jay   George Lorenz

THE WUFO BULLETIN BOARD
10:30 A.M. and 2:30 P.M. daily · WUFO 1080 on Buffalo's radio dial

The WUFO Bulletin Board is a Public Service Presentation of Radio WUFO, aired twice daily, Monday through Saturday in the public's interest. This program announces the activities of the churches, schools, civic groups, and non profit events for social groups and organizations. Any item of a non commercial nature will be welcomed by this program. Announcements will be made daily for approximately a week before the event takes place. There is absolutely no charge for this service. Simply fill in this form with the information requested and mail to the WUFO BULLETIN BOARD, RADIO STATION WUFO, Box 186, Buffalo 21, N.Y. Please type or print your information.

In 1961, station WUFO was founded when the 1080 AM frequency previously used by WINE/WYSL was sold to Leonard Walk. Walk was a pioneer in African American broadcasting and owned a group of Black-formatted stations that included WAMO, Pittsburgh; and WILD, Boston. The call letters WUFO ("WU-FO in Buffalo") were chosen as they provided the rhyming and identification with Buffalo that the owners wanted. The new format was inaugurated on November 2, 1962. Famed Cleveland disc jockey, Eddie O'Jay was the first voice heard, and soon, the station attracted other prominent Black personalities, such as Jimmy Lyons and Frankie Crocker. George Lorenz moved his show to WUFO until he was ready to open his own station, WBLK FM.

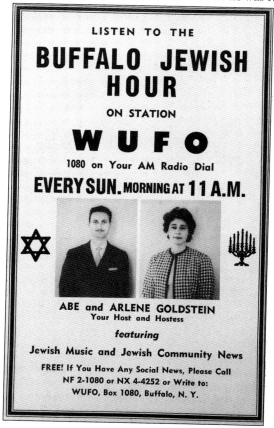

Although programming on WUFO was primarily targeted towards Buffalo's African American community, the station featured the *Buffalo Jewish Hour* every Sunday morning at 11:00 a.m., featuring Jewish music and news presented by Abe and Arlene Goldstein.

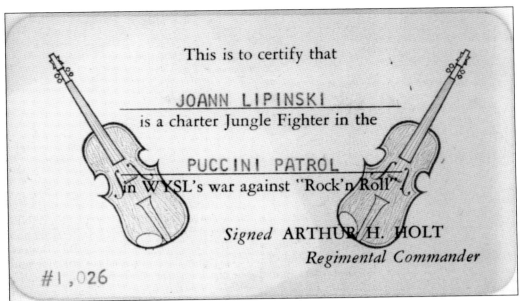

In 1960, broadcaster Gordon McLendon purchased WINE and made a valiant attempt to compete with WKBW's Top 40. Quickly realizing that it was a no-win war, McLendon changed WINE's call letters to WYSL and dropped the Top 40 format in favor of beautiful music. This was Buffalo's anti–rock and roll station, which went so far as to ask young listeners to join a club in support of "good music."

After just one year, WYSL would drop beautiful music and revert back to a Top 40 format, again taking on WKBW in the battle for Top 40 dominance in Buffalo. Fresh jingles, young personalities, and aggressive promotions were used as WYSL geared up to taking on WKBW.

It is the early 1970s, and WYSL has just put together its best chance yet at making a ratings run against WKBW. Pictured from left to right are program director Jack Evans, Roger Christian, Jack Sheridan, Mike O'Shea, Jim Bradley, Rufus Coyote, Kevin O'Connell, Mike Butts, and George Hamburger.

Here is an early logo for the "new" Top 40 WYSL that debuted in 1961.

In 1956, Rochester, New York, broadcasting pioneer Gordon Brown signed onto WNIA from studios located at 2900 Genesee Street in Cheektowaga. With a very limited budget, the station utilized the talents of many young, up-and-coming broadcasters who, to save money on jingles, did not use their real names but "stock" identities like "Jerry Jack," "Tommy Thomas," and "Mike Melody." A tradition each evening at midnight was the playing of Richard Maltby's "Midnight Mood." In 1977, following Brown's passing, the station was sold, and the call letters were changed to WECK in celebration of Buffalo's famous "Beef on Kimmelweck" sandwich.

John "JR" Reid was one of the many "Mike Melody" personalities at WNIA before joining WUSJ, Lockport, in 1964. He is best remembered as the host of "Reid Rocks," an oldies program featuring music from the 1950s and 1960s. Reid, a longtime supporter of the Buffalo Broadcasters Association, passed away in 2022.

Here is WMMJ's "Top Country-Wide Tune" countdown from January 17, 1966. The daily broadcaster lineup included Jack Kelly, Steve Bracken, Bob Yox, and Lee Forester.

Here is a placard for "Happy" Harry Kostrzycki's *Polka Hit Parade* show that aired daily on 1300 WMMJ. The station's call letters represented station owner Stan Jasinski's two daughters, Michelle and Marie Jasinski.

After years of programming, managing, selling, and appearing on countless Buffalo radio stations, Stan Jasinski would be granted his own radio station license in 1965. On January 17 of that year, WMMJ went on the air, broadcasting from studios located in the Buffalo suburb of Lancaster. The station was programed with a mix of country music, as well as polka programs, including those hosted by Stan himself.

In 1947, Ramblin' Lou Schriver was 18 years old and just out of high school. After a brief audition, he was given a 15-minute radio program on WJJL, and his legendary career broadcasting, performing, and promoting country music was born. Over the following decades, Schriver would take his show to WHLD, WWOL, and WMMJ. Finally, in 1970, Stan Jasinski sold WMMJ to Schriver, who changed the call letters to WXRL. Schriver would continue to broadcast on the station until the time of his passing in 2016.

Greg Chwojdak, at right, is pictured with his father "Big" Al Chowjdak. Greg began broadcasting polka music on September 17, 1976, via an experimental audio channel over International Cable. His lively, rock and roll style infused much needed energy into ethnic radio and helped grow a younger polka listening audience. During his over four decades on air, Chwojdak's polka programs have aired on WWOL-AM, WECK-AM and WXRL-AM.

The birthplace of commercial broadcasting in Buffalo was located at 75 West Mohawk Street. On Sunday April 16, 1922, WWT went on the air from a third-floor room inside the headquarters of pioneer Buffalo electrical equipment dealer McCarthy Bros. & Ford. The firm hoped to use the station as a way to encourage sales of home radio sets that they sold out of their downtown showroom. After only two months of intermittent broadcasts, WWT's programming became sporadic due to transmitting issues. By October 2, 1922, Buffalo's first commercial radio station, WWT, officially ceased operations permanently.

Burlesque dancer and vaudeville performer Georgia Sothern poses in 1948 after a promotional appearance on WXRA, Kenmore. Sothern was in Western New York promoting her performances on the James E. Strates Shows Midway.

WBNY's Carl Spavento is pictured with film star Virginia Mayo. Carl's 50-year career in Buffalo broadcasting began in 1942 when he was hired to join WBNY as a staff announcer. In 1947, he was named the station's general manager and signed on WBNY-FM the same year. After decades in management, Carl returned to the airwaves as a news broadcaster at WYSL-AM and WPHD-FM. Spavento retired in 1992.

Discover Thousands of Local History Books Featuring Millions of Vintage Images

Arcadia Publishing, the leading local history publisher in the United States, is committed to making history accessible and meaningful through publishing books that celebrate and preserve the heritage of America's people and places.

Find more books like this at
www.arcadiapublishing.com

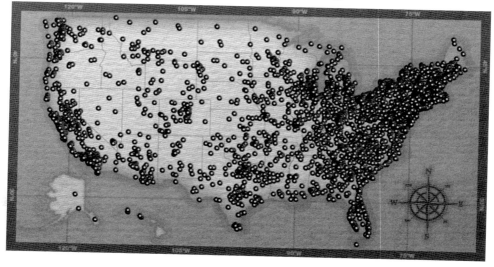

Search for your hometown history, your old stomping grounds, and even your favorite sports team.

Consistent with our mission to preserve history on a local level, this book was printed in South Carolina on American-made paper and manufactured entirely in the United States. Products carrying the accredited Forest Stewardship Council (FSC) label are printed on 100 percent FSC-certified paper.